The Native American Autobiography Series

edited by

H. David Brumble III and Arnold Krupat

Crashing Thunder

The Autobiography of an American Indian

Edited by Paul Radin

*With a foreword and appendix by
Arnold Krupat*

University of Nebraska Press
Lincoln and London

Foreword, appendix, and index copyright 1983 by the University of
Nebraska Press

Manufactured in the United States of America

First Bison Book edition: November 1983
Most recent printing indicated by the first digit below:
1   2   3   4   5   6   7   8   9   10

Library of Congress Cataloging in Publication Data

Blowsnake, Sam.
   Crashing Thunder.
   Reprint. originally published: New York : D. Appleton,
1926.
   Includes index.
   1. Blowsnake, Sam. 2. Winnebago Indians—Biography.
3. Winnebago Indians—Social life and customs.
I. Radin, Paul, 1883–1959. II. Title.
E99.W7B56 1983   970.004'97 [B]   83-6894
ISBN 0-8032-3867-3
ISBN 0-8032-8910-3 (pbk.)

Crashing Thunder: The Autobiography of An American Indian was
first published in 1926 by D. Appleton and Company, New York.

TO
THE MEMORY OF
WILLIAM HALSE RIVERS RIVERS

CONTENTS

FOREWORD
Arnold Krupat

The culmination of Paul Radin's thirteen years of experimentation in the forms of Indian autobiography, *Crashing Thunder: The Autobiography of an American Indian* is perhaps the best known of the many Indian autobiographies gathered by professional anthropologists. Presented to the general public as a contribution to the science of culture, but also for its historical and literary value, *Crashing Thunder* is particularly interesting today precisely for the way in which it blurs the lines once thought to separate the disciplines of anthropology, history, and literature, collapsing the distinctions between fact and interpretation, the objective and the subjective account. A close look at the composition of *Crashing Thunder* reveals what our own post-structuralist age has once again discovered: that no narrative can be transparent upon reality; that the constitution of the "facts" is always a matter of interpretation; and that the very nature of collaborative textual production must be such that not only autobiographical subjects and their culture but autobiographical editors and their culture as well speak in Indian autobiography.

Paul Radin was born in Lodz, Russian Poland, in 1883 and died in New York City in 1959. Brought to the United States as an infant, Radin graduated from the College of the City of New York at the age of nineteen. He went on to Columbia University, where he did work in zoology and wrote a thesis on the embryology of the shark. It was only during later study in Munich, Berlin, and Prague that he became interested in anthropology, returning to Columbia University to take his doctorate under Franz Boas, the putative founder of modern scientific anthropology, in 1911.

Radin did field work among the Winnebagos from 1908 to 1913, the year in which his first attempt at an Indian autobiography appeared. An important document in the history of what would come to be called "personality and culture" in anthropology,

[ix]

Radin's "Personal Reminiscences of a Winnebago Indian" was published in the *Journal of American Folklore,* then edited by Boas. Radin's intention was to "throw . . . light upon the workings of an Indian's brain" and to provide an "inside view of the Indian's emotional life."[1] Boas had emphasized the importance of attention to Native languages, and for the "Personal Reminiscences," Radin published, below the English translation, the Winnebago text as his informant had written it. The translation, he warned, was "liable to an interpretation . . . utterly unjustified by the Winnebago itself" (294).

It was also in 1913 that Radin completed a different sort of ethnographic work: his monumental *The Winnebago Tribe* was the paper accompanying the *Thirty-seventh Annual Report of the Bureau of American Ethnology* for 1915– 16 (it was not actually published until 1923). It was a comprehensive survey of Winnebago history, social and ceremonial organization, and the like. But *The Winnebago Tribe* also contained a number of first-person narratives of various lengths obtained from several Winnebago informants, two of whom were identified as "J.B." and "S.B." "J.B." was Jasper Blowsnake, or Warudjáxega, the subject of the 1913 "Personal Reminiscences," where his name was translated as "terrible thunder-crash"; "S.B." was Jasper's younger brother, Sam Blowsnake, also known as Big Winnebago, whose birth-order name was Hágaga. Sam, not Jasper (the "real" Crashing Thunder), would become the subject of *Crashing Thunder: The Autobiography of an American Indian*. In reference to these first-person narratives, Radin wrote in his preface that "throughout the work, the Indian has been allowed to tell the facts in his own way."[2] "It has been the aim of the author," he added, "to separate as definitely as possible his own comments from the data obtained" (47). It was precisely upon such a separation, indeed, that Radin's conception of the scienticity of his autobiographical work depended, for Radin shared Boas's hypostasization of the distinction between fact and interpretation, between the objective and the subjective presentation.

In 1920, Radin published a second Indian autobiography, "The Autobiography of a Winnebago Indian." This was the story of Sam Blowsnake, identified in the text only as S.B.; it is this text on which *Crashing Thunder* would be based. The "Autobiography" also appeared under scientific auspices and in the Boasian milieu,

Foreword

in the *University of California Publications in American Archaeology and Ethnology*, edited by Alfred Kroeber, who had been the first to take a doctorate in anthropology with Boas at Columbia. This text, Radin announced in his introduction, is "likely to throw more light on the workings of the mind and emotions of primitive man than any amount of speculation from a sophisticated ethnologist or ethnological theorist."[3] Radin attests to his objectivity in the production of this text with the statement that "no attempt of any kind was made to influence him [S.B.] in the selection of the particular facts which he chose to present" (2).

Before reworking the "Autobiography" for *Crashing Thunder,* Radin once ventured outside the confines of science into what was ostensibly fiction. In 1922, he prepared a chapter called "Thunder-Cloud, a Winnebago Shaman, Relates and Prays," for Elsie Clews Parsons's *American Indian Life.* Parsons, also a student of Boas (who contributed to the book; Kroeber wrote the introduction), wanted to broaden the appeal of anthropological material concerning the Indian beyond the community of professional researchers but still to retain the accuracy of science. Her way to avoid what she called merely bringing "Fenimore Cooper up to date" was to have prominent anthropologists write fictional accounts of aspects of the cultures they had studied.[4] Most of these took the form of biographical or autobiographical narratives. Despite what Kroeber called the "fictional form of presentation devised by the editor," Radin's "Thunder-Cloud" (along with other of the characters in Parsons's book) was "real" enough.[5] Thunder-Cloud had made an extensive appearance in the 1913 "Personal Reminiscences," he had told of his fasting experiences in *The Winnebago Tribe,* and he had received mention in the "Autobiography." The monologue ascribed to him in Parsons's book is hardly a work of fiction; rather, it is a composite of two first-person narratives Radin had recorded for *The Winnebago Tribe,* "Thundercloud's fasting experience," and "How an Indian shaman cures his patients."

Finally, in 1926, Radin published *Crashing Thunder: The Autobiography of an American Indian.* This is, as I have said, the life history not of Jasper Blowsnake, Warudjáxega, "terrible thunder-crash," the "real" Crashing Thunder, but of his younger brother, Sam. In his introduction to Sam's 1920 "Autobiography," Radin had told his readers he had made no attempt to influence his informant "in the selection of the particular facts of his life which he chose to present" (2) and that "so far as could be ascertained the Indian wrote the autobiography in two consecutive sessions in a syllabary now commonly used among the Winnebago" (2). Radin did not, however, publish the original as he had in 1913, but only his own translation, made "on the basis of a rendition from his interpreter, Oliver Lamere, of Winnebago, Nebraska" (2). In the preface to *Crashing Thunder*, Radin gives a somewhat fuller account of "Crashing Thunder's" production of the autobiography, one which, in its acknowledgment of Radin's persistence in overcoming "Crashing Thunder's" reluctance to write his life, complicates his claims to noninfluence. Radin's account in *The Road of Life and Death* of how he obtained from Jasper Blowsnake the Winnebago Medicine Rite, and his curious relation to Mountain Wolf Woman, sister of Sam and Jasper Blowsnake, in 1958, suggest that this most learned and urbane scientist could be relatively unsophisticated in his understanding of what might constitute influence upon an informant.[6] Nancy Lurie notes that surely "an element of coercion was involved with . . . Crashing Thunder."[7] But apart from the indirect influence Radin (like any other anthropologist) may have exerted upon his informants, there is the direct influence he unquestionably exerted upon the final text of their autobiographies.

Although it is based on the 1920 "Autobiography," *Crashing Thunder* is very different from it. The 92 pages of the "Autobiography" have been expanded to the 203 pages of *Crashing Thunder* by the addition, as Radin says, of "certain Things . . . that Crashing Thunder had told me on previous occasions."[8] Part II of the "Autobiography," called by Radin "My Father's Teachings," appears in *Crashing Thunder* not as a separate section, but variously distributed throughout the narrative; instead of the 351 footnotes Radin provided for the "Autobiography," there are only 32 footnotes to *Crashing Thunder*. In the "Autobiography" a great number of words appeared in parentheses. Radin had initiated this practice in his translation of the "Personal Reminiscences," where, he had explained, the parenthetical words were his own addition to the text to "complete the sense" (294). There are no parenthetical words in *Crashing Thunder*, however, and while this does free up the movement of the narrative, it also tends to obscure the editor's participation in the production of the text.

Foreword

For the changes I have noted between the "Autobiography" and *Crashing Thunder* are all the result of Radin's determination. My point here is not to criticize him for making those changes, but only to demonstrate that they exist and that they have an important bearing upon our interpretation and understanding of the text. Even if we grant that both the "Autobiography" and *Crashing Thunder* present the "facts" as told by an Indian, with no intentional attempt on the part of the anthropologist to influence him (this would be to grant a lot, perhaps too much), we would still have to remark that the "same" "facts" appear in very different forms. But this is only to remind ourselves that ethnographies, like histories, and as well as fictional narratives, are texts, and that no text can innocently represent the "order of things" independently of the orders of language. Radin's selection from and arrangement of the available materials, his decisions in matters of translation—indeed, every aspect of its mode of presentation—make *Crashing Thunder* an interpretation of a life, one that is, in its turn, in need of interpretation.

For example, in reworking the "Autobiography" for *Crashing Thunder*, Radin revised his earlier translation, ostensibly in the interest of achieving greater accuracy and authenticity. He may well have achieved this aim; yet some of his retranslations seem more artistically than scientifically effective. I will let one instance stand for many. (A fuller discussion of textual matters may be found in the Appendix.) The second paragraph of the "Autobiography" reads, "I was a good-tempered boy, it is said. At boyhood my father told me to fast and I obeyed. In the winter every morning I would crush charcoal and blacken my face with it. I would arise very early and do it. As soon as the sun rose I would go outside and sit looking at the sun and I would cry to the spirits" (3). Here is how this passage appears in *Crashing Thunder*: "I have been told that I was a good-tempered child. During childhood my father told me to fast and I obeyed him. Throughout the winter, every morning, I would get up very early, crush charcoal, and then blacken my face with it. As soon as the sun rose would I go outside and there gazing steadily at the sun, make my prayer to the spirits, crying" (1).

Syntax and diction have been modified in accord with—if not Victorian, at least pre-modernist—concepts of stylistic elegance. The rhythm has been changed; the parataxis of the first has, in general, yielded to a more nearly hypertactic style in the second. In particular, the inversion ("would I" for "I would"); the substitution of the more meditative-reverent "gazing" for the neutral "looking"; the addition of the descriptive, "steadily"; and the rising inflection of the participial terminative, all seem strong markers of a literary motivation.[9] Another change in the direction, as it would initially appear, of greater literariness, may, however, be intended to increase the scienticity, that is, the ostensible objectivity, of *Crashing Thunder*. In 1920, Radin translated S.B.'s concluding remarks as "This is the work that was assigned to me. This is the end of it" (67). But in 1926, we have "This is the work predestined for me to do. This is the end of it" (203). Here a change is introduced, it would seem, both for its dramatic effect and for its support of Radin's scientific stance of nondirective objectivity. In any case, the issue of literalness and literariness in translation is everywhere important in *Crashing Thunder*, as it is in the life history generally.

This is not, however, to legitimize the debate whether *Crashing Thunder* is more nearly a work of science or of art, a debate that has mistakenly persisted to the present day. In 1961, Ruth Underhill, a fine ethnologist and collector of Indian autobiography, wrote that in *Crashing Thunder* "Radin was artist rather than ethnologist."[10] A different opinion was expressed by L. L. Langness in a broad survey of the life history field in anthropology. Langness, in 1965, pronounced *Crashing Thunder*, in effect, a masterpiece of early science, "the beginning of truly rigorous work in the field of biography by professional anthropologists."[11] Langness repeated this estimate in 1981.[12]

Such a debate mistakes the nature of narrative in general and of Indian autobiography in particular. For it is of the nature of narrative always to be a textualization of the "facts," never the "facts" themselves; thus, as George Marcus and Dick Cushman have argued, for ethnography (as for history), "rhetorical analysis is prior to an evaluation of truth claims."[13] The particular selection from and arrangement of the "facts," as well as the language in which they are presented, may appear more literal or more literary to a given reader, more useful for the purposes of science or of art. And this decision depends as much upon the reader's determination to read through the text to a world beyond or to remain within the textual system of signification, upon the reader's conception of

Foreword

what constitutes a "fact," as it does upon the given text itself. Further, because Indian autobiography as a genre of American writing is constituted by the principle of bicultural composite composition, as "art" or as "science" it must always speak not only of its Native American subjects and their culture but of its Euramerican editors and their culture as well, and it must speak in ways that bear the pressures of the different modes of production, "aesthetic" or "scientific," of the two cultures.

The conventions of autobiography in Euramerican culture require, to be sure, that nothing be purely invented; but, as I have tried to indicate, autobiography cannot escape the general problematics of narrative. Nonetheless, just because autobiography is bound by the real, although we cannot accept it as "true" in some simple way, it can make itself legitimately available to scientific usage in ways that pure fiction cannot; "an evaluation of truth claims" is an appropriate step in the analysis of autobiography in ways that it is not in the analysis of a fictional text.

All I have been saying urges us to see Radin's autobiographical work with the Winnebagos, and *Crashing Thunder* most of all, differently from the way in which he saw it. To see it differently, of course, is to value it differently—but in no way to deny its immense value. Radin's work may be read for the light it sheds on the mind of the Indian and of the culture to which he belonged; it may be read, too, for the light it sheds on Radin's mind and the social-scientific culture of the first quarter of the twentieth century to which he belonged. There are other ways in which it might be read; indeed, I hope that this reprint of *Crashing Thunder* will encourage the sort of hermeneutical activity appropriate to it, precisely positing some of the contexts in which it means most. *Crashing Thunder* has much to say to students of anthropology, of history, and of literature, as well as to the general reader who is curious about Indian lives and the attempts of non-Indians to understand them.

Notes

1. Paul Radin, "Personal Reminiscences of a Winnebago Indian," *Journal of American Folklore* 26 (1913): 293. Further references to this work are documented in the text. Radin, in fact,

means "mind" here, not "brain," and he corrected himself a few years later in a similar formulation. He could not mean "brain" without contradicting scientific anthropology's central premise, the cultural explanation of cultural things. Radin shared Boas's determination that race and physiology were inadequate explanations of cultural variation.

2. Paul Radin, *The Winnebago Tribe* (Washington: Government Printing Office, 1923), p. 47. Further references to this work are documented in the text.

3. Paul Radin, *The Autobiography of a Winnebago Indian* (New York: Dover, 1963), p. 2. Further references are to this edition and will be documented in the text. Original publication, as noted, was in the *University of California Publications in American Archaeology and Ethnology* 16 (April 15, 1920): 381–473.

4. Elsie Clews Parsons, *American Indian Life* (1922; reprinted Lincoln: University of Nebraska Press, 1967), p. 2.

5. A. L. Kroeber, Introduction to Parsons, *American Indian Life*, p. 13. For the "real" subjects of these anthropologists' "fictions," see H. David Brumble, *An Annotated Bibliography of American Indian and Eskimo Autobiographies* (Lincoln: University of Nebraska Press, 1981), #462.

6. In his Introduction to *The Road of Life and Death: A Ritual Drama of the American Indian* (New York: Bollingen-Pantheon, 1945), Radin tells of pursuing the reluctant Jasper Blowsnake with a horse and wagon (pp. 44 ff.). Later, Radin visited Nancy O. Lurie and Mountain Wolf Woman when they were at work on the latter's autobiography in 1958. According to Lurie, "Paul Radin questioned [Mountain Wolf Woman] about peyote before we reached this point in her account. Since he spoke of her brother's first vision in what she considered an offhand manner, she did not want to speak of a matter of such deep emotional significance to herself. Dr. Radin expressed mild amusement that her brother's first vision had included frightening snakes, so she confined herself to telling him a funny incident in regard to an early peyote experience." Nancy O. Lurie, ed., *Mountain Wolf Woman, Sister of Crashing Thunder: The Autobiography of a Winnebago Indian* (Ann Arbor: University of Michigan Press, 1961), p. 127. Working some thirty years after Radin, Lurie was, herself, particularly sensitive to and aware of the complexities of "influence." Radin's own sensitivity to this issue, such as it may have been, seems fairly

Foreword

illustrated by some remarks he made only a year after the publication of *Crashing Thunder*. In his preface to *Primitive Man as Philosopher* (New York: D. Appleton and Co., 1927), he acknowledged that, for all their commitment to objectivity," ethnologists often find it necessary to give what are simply their own impressions and interpretations." But this seemed to him not fit subject for concern, for, he continued, "I must confess myself to have had frequent recourse to impressions and interpretations, which I have then sought to illustrate by appropriate examples. But I realize quite clearly *how easy it is to obtain appropriate examples,* and mine, I hope, have been chosen judiciously" (p. xi, my emphasis).

7. Lurie, *Mountain Wolf Woman*, p. 93.

8. Paul Radin, *Crashing Thunder: The Autobiography of an American Indian* (New York: D. Appleton and Co., 1926), p. xi. Further references are documented in the text.

9. Nancy Lurie's comments on these matters are particularly valuable. According to Lurie, "Radin was inspired to try to capture more of the eloquence of the Winnebago text in the 'liberties' he took with the translation as received from Lamere. Gazing probably comes closer than looking, e.g. The 'would I,' in the example you [A.K.] give, might be a better choice than 'I would.' Pronouns are all bound forms, infixed into the verb and even the word 'sit' in the first version is a bound form of the verb, in effect gazing-while-sitting, all one verb with the pronoun and mood also infixed. At this time, of course, it would be hard to say whether Radin was being more 'literary' in somewhat outmoded Euroamerican terms or more 'literary' in trying to convey the Winnebago delight in speech as an art. . . . 'it is said' is probably closer to the Winnebago original than 'I have been told.' It might even have been a•i•re•na, 'they say,' which is a common term in such narrative statements. The sentence in Winnebago probably was boy, good tempered, I was, it is said. Even that doesn't do it literally because of the pronouns" (personal communication).

10. Ruth Underhill, Foreword to Lurie, *Mountain Wolf Woman*, p. ix.

11. L. L. Langness, *The Life History in Anthropological Science* (New York: Holt, Rinehart, and Winston, 1965), p. 7. Just how "rigorous" Radin actually was in his composition of *Crashing Thunder* is an open question. See the Appendix to this volume for

a fuller consideration of this matter.

12. L. L. Langness and Gelya Frank, *Lives: An Anthropological Approach to Biography* (Novato, Calif.: Chandler and Sharp, 1981), p. 18.

13. George E. Marcus and Dick Cushman, "Ethnographies as Texts," *Annual Review of Anthropology* 11 (1982): 56 n.

PREFACE

For most individuals the American Indian still possesses a tremendous appeal, an appeal which, in a manner, constitutes one of the great obstacles to our properly understanding him. It has been that way since the days of the discovery of the continent. Then it was the gold and the pearls that exercised a magical fascination; to-day it is the belief that somehow, in some way, the Indians are still living in that delightful half-Arcadian condition of simplicity after which so many souls still yearn, particularly those individuals who dwell in the city. Nothing is gained by calling these people sentimentalists. We should always remember that from the time Spanish chroniclers began writing their accounts of El Dorado and the quaint peoples with the still quainter customs who dwelt there, the Indian has been a symbol for youth and freedom of expression, for freedom from the shackles of civilized constraint. Like Siegfried he knew the language of the birds and patted Nature kindly on the back. A vast literature has grown up on this symbolism of the Indian, particularly in France.

It seems almost sacrilege to trifle with this vision or to question it, and the first result of a so-called scientific inquiry is bound to leave a very bad sensation of nightmare. That is, of course, the terrible price all sentimentalists must pay for the undiluted pleasure they have had of rocking themselves into a fictitious bliss from which they are to be rudely and unceremoniously awakened. Yet this seems to me exceedingly bad sportsmanship, to say the least, and an exceedingly erroneous conception of romance. There is, in fact, infinitely more romance—if it is romance we are seeking, and most of us are—in trying to obtain an approximately accurate account of what this Indian of our childhood imagination actually is, how he thinks, feels, reacts, adapts himself to the varying conditions of life, than in rehearsing all the scenes of Chateaubriand and Cooper.

But having set ourselves this task of discovering what the real Indian is like, we are immediately surrounded by difficulties. One of the greatest drawbacks in the study of a primitive people is, in fact, the difficulty of obtaining an inside view of their culture from their own lips and by their own initiative. Let no investigator flatter himself: a native informant is at best interested in merely satisfying the demands of the investigator. The limitations thus imposed as regards the nature and the extent of the knowledge obtained are still further increased by the circumstances in which the knowledge is generally imparted, circumstances of a nature tending to destroy practically all the subjective values associated with the particular ritual, myth, etc., that is being narrated.

How can this fundamental defect be remedied?

Preface

There is only one way—to have a native himself give the account in his own mother tongue. The problem then resolves itself into finding the native. That is the task I set myself and through a piece of good luck I succeeded in accomplishing it. As the manner of its accomplishment is an interesting and illuminating story in itself, I hope I shall be excused for telling it in some detail.

In the year 1909 I commenced field investigations among the Winnebago Indians living on the Nebraska side of the Missouri River, about twenty-five miles south of Sioux City, Iowa. These Indians had the reputation of being fairly conservative. Perhaps the fact that a Presbyterian mission had in seventeen years succeeded in converting only one family, and a family which then unkindly died without leaving issue, may bear this out.

Among these Indians there lived a family named Blow Snake, consisting of a father and a fair number of children all grown up. Two of these were men quite well known in the tribe for a variety of reasons. These two became my principal informants. They had lived the most exciting of lives, for to the usual round of adventures that fall to the lot of most Indians of that region now, they had added a murder and a conversion, the murder first and the conversion afterwards. The older of the two seemed to be by far the more gifted. His memory was simply prodigious. He recounted to me a ceremony which took him two months, working practically six hours a day, to tell me. But what is more to the point here is that he wove my presence among the Winnebago just then, into the whole fabric of his life. I was the preordained one who had sensed what was the proper time to come to the Winnebago, and this legend he diligently disseminated among all his relatives and subsequently embodied in certain autobiographical snatches I obtained from him. It was from him that I obtained a short sketch of reminiscences which, short as they were, threw more light on the real Indian than any of the more elaborate things I had collected in the usual external fashion which is the pride of scientific procedure among ethnologists.

It was from the perusal of these "reminiscences" that the idea developed within me of getting a real autobiography, and having heard vaguely of the adventures and tribulations of Crashing Thunder, the younger brother of the family, which seemed to bear all the earmarks of a true rake's progress, I approached him about the matter, to receive a meaningless affirmative reply. For three years he eluded me on one pretext or another until temporary poverty induced him to consent to write down in a syllabary now in use among the Winnebago the fascinating tale of his life. I remember very well how worried he was after he had finally consented. After writing the first part he came to me at midnight, in a very nervous condition, saying that he did not care to proceed because what he had to say would not look nice if white people subsequently read it. When his fears were appeased he continued and within forty-eight hours the whole manuscript was done.

It is this manuscript translated literally that is here presented. No changes of any kind have been introduced. Certain things, however, that Crashing Thunder had told me on previous occasions, which, for that reason, he merely mentions in the autobiography proper, I have inserted in their proper places. Everything in this manuscript comes directly from him and was told in the original and in the first person. It is needless for me to insist that I in no way influenced him either directly or indirectly in any way.

Some years ago the autobiography proper was published with annotations as an ethnological document in the University of California Series in American Archæology and Ethnology under the title "The Autobiography of a Winnebago Indian" (Volume XVI, Number 7). I gratefully acknowledge the generosity of the authorities of the University Press in permitting this reissue for a wider audience, in part retranslated and considerably enlarged by the additions mentioned above.

P. R.

INTRODUCTION

THE common-sense man, the man in the street, has always been good-naturedly skeptical of the academically trained scholar, particularly when the latter chose to discuss the subject of man and his moods and to make generalizations concerning phases of life and thought that, from the very nature of the case, he could only remotely understand. The glamour that for so long a time hung about the educated man and his unlimited capacity for understanding everything has slowly but surely evaporated in the last generation. We are all now quite willing to admit that the economist and the sociologist, the psychologist and the historian are capable of making—and do frequently make—the most ludicrous and appalling mistakes as soon as they find themselves compelled to deal with man himself in all his vagaries, his inconsistencies, and his lack of direction. Perhaps it is this more than any other single factor that has led to the popular characterization of history as a pleasant, amiable, but wholly imaginative record of man as he never existed. We can fill our libraries and public archives with as many details as we wish and yet in no way improve on the situation or alter the fundamental distortion and ludicrousness of the average presentation of history. The real man, man as he actually is, will never be revealed to us in this manner.

There is nothing new in this criticism. Most of us have always suspected that such was the case, and have, as a corrective, instinctively sought refuge in the letters and autobiographies of men of their time. But letters and autobiographies written by citizens of such complicated civilizations as are those of our own time, in their turn, represent most frequently, conscious or at best unconscious distortions of the people who wrote them. Our notions of convention and propriety effectually bar any true revelation. No man who regards his thoughts, feelings, and actions of sufficient importance for him to note them down in a diary or an autobiography, ever admits to himself or to the world for whom he is writing that his life has not been a unified whole or that it did not gradually lead to a proper and early heralded climax. Can any one picture to himself a man, in our civilization, writing an autobiography in which he frankly admitted that his life had ended in an anticlimax or that he had throughout been but a reed driven the way the wind listeth? And yet many of us, be it confessed, are so driven, even some of those who write autobiographies.

The value and significance of the autobiography that follows does not simply lie in the fact that it is a document absolutely unique of its kind—the only account that has ever been obtained from a so-called "primitive" man—but in the fact that this particular individual took his task literally and attempted to give an absolutely and bewilderingly honest account of his life. He apparently proceeded from an assumption, strange to us, that however damaging to a man's reputation his actions and thoughts may have been, no amount of blinking can possibly do away with them. Now this American Indian did something, in its way, even more remarkable: he never confused his reputation or his own explanations of himself with his real self. He did not, for a moment, fall into the error of the writers of most of our own *Confessions*. No, he most emphatically does not beat his breast and cry, "Father, I have sinned," or exclaim, on the other hand, "Look how wicked I have been!" Far from it. Apology is the very last thing he has in mind. At all times he accepts and approves of himself. We are taken into his confidence on the very first page. There he informs us in the most matter-of-fact manner that shortly before he was born his mother had been told by a very prominent member of the tribe that she was about to give birth to a man of no ordinary importance! Had he been as unconsciously dishonest as the heroes of most of our autobiographies he would have made this the theme of his life and he would have attempted to prove or disprove this prophecy.

He does nothing of the kind. When he was but a small boy, so he tells us, he heard what had been prophesied about him. He accepts and tries to impress the world around him with its truth, but he sees no reason for dwelling upon it to the utter exclusion of all the other pertinent facts about his life. This is all the more remarkable in view of the fact that he was a somewhat unusual man both in character and in intellect. Few people in any community, civilized or uncivilized, have ever had so full an experience with life in all its ramifications. Benvenuto Cellini's life was drab in comparison. Yet no man has ever so successfully refrained from dramatizing these experiences in the interest of an imaginary audience as did this untutored "savage." He never forgets what the actual facts were. At the most tense moment of his life, when he has unwittingly become converted to a new religion and seen visions of the most beatific kind, he refuses to dramatize, and allows a most gloriously opportune moment to sink into an uninteresting anticlimax merely because it happened to be an anticlimax.

The rhythm of his life, like that of the generality of mankind, was a succession of climaxes and anticlimaxes, and so he portrays it. He began his life with a lie and it was rounded by murder and a conversion. Much of it was spent in sexual debauch and in drunkenness. Pleasures and intense sufferings were also his. His favorite brother is killed, murdered. He longs for revenge and in despair desires death. Like so many people before and after him he seeks forgetfulness in the cup. Yet he has the amazing and disconcerting honesty to admit that after a while he got so fond of drinking that he forgot all about his primary object.

He gets delirium tremens and shares with Burns the rare good fortune of seeing ghosts drunk. But his ghosts are more terrifying. They are the ghosts of men whom he had known very well and they are on horse-back singing a song with a very old theme: "We all must die some time: so what value is there to anything."

Upon becoming sober he finds that he has added one more experience to his already rich store: he has become a poet and his song a favorite drinking song. Subsequently, at his conversion, he sees God, identifies himself with God, with the soul and with thought itself. He reaches the startling philosophical conclusion—proceeding from one deduction to another—that he is his thought and from this again he draws the perfectly logical inference that, though still living, his corporeal affairs are over. When he recovers from his hallucination he continues as though nothing had happened. He does not become insane nor does he confuse his hallucination with reality.

As a child he was markedly non-suggestible and he afterwards passes successively from the rôle of a man about town to that of a pimp, a thief, a murderer, and a coward, finally to develop into an excellent philosopher and something of a moralist. And yet he always feels himself the same, no better or worse at the end than at the beginning. He passes no judgment, he makes no evaluations on what he has done. In his own eyes he is no better when he finally succeeds in living up to a certain standard of self-restraint that would have made him a hero in any standard European biography than he was when, to save himself from imprisonment he, in the most selfish fashion conceivable, betrays his companions who had participated in a murder which he had planned and for which he got all the glory. The question of good and bad simply does not present itself to him, because the task he had set himself did not entail the passing of judgments but the giving of as an accurate account of his life as was possible for him to give.

It would be both incorrect and stupid to imagine that he was either morally blunted or unintelligent or that he did not have many of those half-mystical strivings that so many of us have. All his life, in fact, can be said to have been spent in the search of an experience which his marked non-suggestibility when a child prevented him from then obtaining. The fundamental religious experience of every member of the tribe to which he belonged was obtained in early youth. It consisted of fasting, of retiring at night to some lonely and inaccessible spot where one could commune undisturbed with the deities. Most youths got it. It was something of a disgrace not to. Yet he did not. In spite of his dishonestly persuading his father that he had been properly blessed, he never deluded himself about the matter. He always felt the stigma attached to his failure to experience what all the others had obtained, and in his inconsistent fashion he tried to find some substitute. When he finally got the experience he had been seeking, although it had come to him in the most devious and unexpected manner, he recognized it at once, was satisfied, and became a good man, even from the normal Christian standpoint.

Introduction

A man to whom this could have happened was clearly not blunted either spiritually or morally. He was merely true to the task he had voluntarily imposed upon himself when he decided to write an account of his life, when he refused to see running through it a purpose from which he had never deviated and which had blotted out everything else. His final conversion and spiritual and moral regeneration are consequently to him neither a reaction against his vices nor the ending of a long continued inward search. It is just an incident happening to come last.

Here is a theme out of which a dozen heroes could have been forged. Our author, however, makes no pretense at being one. He consistently and objectively pictures himself as never rising superior to any situation, not even toward the end. Wherever in life there was any temptation to which he could succumb, he succumbed to it. Even at the turning-point of his life, before he eats the medicine that is to lead to his conversion, he frankly and acutely observes, "I thought I was fooling them and they thought they were converting me!" Life and his own emotions and moods buffeted him about incessantly and no consistent direction is anywhere visible. What neither life nor his own nature could do, however, was to delude him into believing that he was any other than what he was, or that he had had an experience when he knew he had not had it.

Herein lies the fundamental value of this document for all those who are interested in the *comédie humaine,* whether professionally or unprofessionally. Here is a man with an unusual capacity for articulate expression and fortunately free from our traditional conventions and proprieties, setting before himself the task of pleasing a sympathetic white man by writing down for him what he regarded as significant and important in his life. What facts is he going to select? Is he going to begin with the last act and work backwards, that is, is he going to attempt to show how all the experiences in his life have led to the crowning achievement of his forty-fifth year? As we have pointed out, he had ample reasons for so considering it, for he did obtain at the age of forty-five that experience he had missed in his youth. But he is too good a psychologist to humbug himself into any such belief.

Accordingly he begins with the beginning. He describes his birth with meticulous care, and he does the same for his early childhood and the formation of certain personal habits which for us seem trivial, such as how he acquired the habit of eating fast or how he acquired the habit of taking the blanket away from people with whom he slept. His life to him means something very specific, and he describes the significant stirrings of early childhood and youth with an insight and accuracy that would do justice to the finest psychological novelist. He indicates the precise time when he began to have memory of things and afterwards the first stirrings of sex. He very delightfully states when the desire arose within him of "making himself pleasing to the opposite sex." From the beginning, as I have repeatedly pointed out, he shows an unusual insistence in separating what he has actually experienced from what he should have experienced. We saw above that when he failed to get into *rapport* with the spirits during his youthful fasting, he states so unhesitatingly, although he strove hard to obtain the desired communion with the deities. Not strong-charactered enough to admit his failure, he deceives his parents. In the same way he confesses to being anything but a success with the girls in his early days. Here again, however, he cannot resist the temptation of pretending to be very successful.

Psychologically and humanly, what is so interesting here is not so much the fact that he knows the difference between truth and desirable social fiction, but that he never becomes a cynic. He escapes this because there is nothing he is hiding, and cynicism therefore is quite unnecessary. He needs no defense mechanism. He is giving a description of his life and it so happened that in his life, owing to certain weaknesses in his character, outwardly pretense had to rule over truth. Due, however, to his inward honesty, it never did. How, in fact, he managed not to confuse the two more than he did is somewhat of a mystery to me. It bespeaks a man with many facets to his personality and at the same time a personality which itself was markedly unintegrated. It is to this same multiple personality that we shall have to ascribe also his amazing faculty for living himself into the particular period of life which he is at the moment describing. Although he

wrote down the autobiography when he was a stanch
adherent of a new religious sect which had definitely
broken with the old cultural background, this in no
way interfered with the accuracy and the sympathetic
penetration with which he described the old background. Never does he forget himself and inveigh
against it. When he describes his childhood he is a
child, his youth a youth, the Medicine Dance a member
of that fraternity, and finally when he describes the
new religion it is as a stanch adherent. Everything in
its proper place and time.

Thus he passes through life, or, better, life passes
through him—lying, boasting, swaggering, stealing,
murdering, fornicating, interpreting dreams in the most
approved Jungian fashion, and finally philosophizing
and adding a new proof of the truth of the Trinity—
consistently lying to the world about him and never
lying to himself. Always very kind, he was throughout
life unable to resist the appeal of his kindred, particularly of the more immediate members of his family.
He ends his account fittingly and in the most approved
style of Voltaire. He, too, like Candide, was going to
settle down. He was happy and his wife had a new
baby.

All we have thus far discussed relates directly to the
personal and human implications of this amazing revelation of a "child of nature." But there are other aspects
just as important. Its value as an ethnological and
psychological document need not be stressed, for that
is apparent at every turn. It seems to me, however,

that its significance for the student of religions and religious psychology cannot be placed too high. Whether he has made a correct analysis or not, he here gives us his version of his conversion with the most remarkable detail. We see his struggle, the reasons for his resistance and the strong urge to please his family, and finally we see his conversion in all the completeness and absoluteness of a revelation.

In conclusion may I hope that this document, because of its authenticity and its freedom from all outside influence, will play its rôle in dissipating once and for all the erroneous notion that still persists—that primitive peoples are incapable of an objective and analytical presentation of facts, that they can draw no clear line between truth and illusion, between hallucination and phantasy-dreaming on the one hand, and the objective world on the other.

PAUL RADIN

§1. *Early Childhood*

Father and mother had four children and after I was born. An uncle of my mother named White Cloud spoke to her before I was born and told her, "You are about to give birth to a child who will not be an ordinary individual." These were the words he addressed to her. It was then that my mother gave birth to me. As soon as I was born, indeed as I was being washed—as my neck was being washed—I laughed out loudly.

I have been told [1] that I was a good-tempered child.

During childhood my father told me to fast and I obeyed him. Throughout the winter, every morning, I would get up very early, crush charcoal, and then blacken my face with it. As soon as the sun rose would I go outside and there gazing steadily at the sun, make my prayer to the spirits, crying. [2]

[1] Whenever the writer refers to events that happened before his time or before he could remember things, he always uses the quotative, "it is said."

[2] This refers to the custom of fasting of which many examples will be found later on. Among the Winnebago and many culturally related tribes, every person, male and female, was expected, between the ages of five and twelve, to seek communion with some supernatural spirit and the spirit so obtained was supposed to grant the suppliant certain powers and in general preside over his destinies throughout life. The proper manner of approaching this ordeal was to blacken one's face with charcoal and retire at night to some semi-deserted place at some distance from the house and there pray-

Thus I acted up to the time that I have memory of things.

In those days there were not many white people living near us as to-day. My father went out hunting continually. The lodge in which we lived was covered with rush mattings, with reed mattings spread over the floor. After hunting for some time in one place we would move to another. My father, mother, older sisters, and older brothers, all carried the packs. Thus we would spend our time until the spring of the year and then in the spring we would again move in order to live near some stream where father could hunt muskrats, mink, otter, and beaver.

In the summer we always returned to Black River Falls, Wisconsin. Here all the Indians gathered after they had given their feasts. Then we picked berries. When picking berries my father used to buy me gum so that I should not be able to eat any of the berries. I managed however to eat berries and chew gum at the same time. After a while I learned to chew tobacco and then I did not eat the berries while picking them. Later on I got to like tobacco very much and I probably used up more money in buying tobacco than would have been the value of the berries had I eaten them.

---

ing and crying to await the coming of the spirit. Among the Winnebago, and probably among many other tribes, it was customary for the parents or grandparents, to prepare the children specifically for what was likely to happen; to inform them how to recognize the approach of the spirit and, what was more to the point, to teach them how to distinguish a good from a bad spirit.

[2]

Early Childhood

In the fall of the year we would pick cranberries. When the hunting season was open, I would begin to fast again.

This was my life for a number of years.

After a while we bought a pony on which we used to pack all our belongings whenever we moved our camp. In addition three of us would ride on top of the pack. Sometimes my mother and sometimes my father drove the pony.

After I had grown a little older and taller all of us brothers would fast together. My father would indeed repeatedly urge us to fast. "Do not be afraid of the burnt remains of the lodge center-pole," he would say to us.[3] "Whatever are the true possessions of men, the apparel of men and the gift of doctoring—all these things that are spread out before you—do try and obtain one of them." [4] Thus he would speak to us.

I would then take a piece of charcoal, crush it and blacken my face and he would be very grateful to me.

I would at first break my fast at noon but then gradually I began to fast all night. From the fall of the year until spring I would fast until nightfall and then eat. After a while I trained myself to pass the night without eating and after that I was able to go two nights and days without taking any food. Then my mother went to the woods at some distance from the

[3] Symbolical manner of describing the crushed charcoal with which fasters must blacken their faces.

[4] By "possessions of men" he means mainly that knowledge which will make a man honored and respected in his community; and by "apparel of men," he means power and ability.

[3]

village and there she built me a small lodge in which I and my elder brother were to remain whenever we had to fast through the whole night. At this fasting-place we used to play and before we were really able to spend a night at this particular place we moved away.

After a time I passed from this stage of childhood to another. I now began to use a bow and arrow and I spent my day at play, shooting arrows.

It was at about this time also that I found out that my mother had been told just before I was born that she was about to give birth to a child who would not be an ordinary being, and from then on I felt that I must be an uncommon person.

At about the same time my elder sister married a very holy man. My parents gave her in marriage to him. He was a shaman and he thought a great deal of me.

§2. *My Brother-in-Law Thunder Cloud*

My brother-in-law was named Thunder Cloud. It is said that he was living his third life as a human being.[5]

This is his account:

I once lived with a small group of Indians numbering about twenty camps. When I had grown up to be a lad, although still not large enough to handle a gun, a war-party attacked us and killed us all. I did not know, however, that I had been killed. I thought that I was running about as usual until I saw a heap of bodies on the ground and mine among them. No one was there to bury us, so there we lay and rotted.

My ghost was taken to the place where the sun sets. There I lived with an old couple. The land of the spirits is an excellent place and the people have the best of times. If you desire to go anywhere all that you have to do is to wish yourself there and you reach it. While there I thought I would like to come to the earth again so the old man with whom I was staying said to me, "My son, did you not speak about wanting to go to the earth again?" I had as

[5] The belief in reincarnation is very widespread among the Winnebago. It is generally believed that if any child resembles some deceased individual he is that individual reincarnated. Not every person, however, can become reincarnated. This is a privilege that belongs only to the more prominent people and to the members of the most sacred of Winnebago ceremonies, the Medicine Dance.

[5]

a matter of fact only thought of it yet he knew what I wanted. Then he said to me, "You can go but you must ask our chief first." Then I went and told the chief of the village of my desire, and he said to me, "You may go and obtain your revenge upon the people who killed your relatives."

Then I was brought down to earth. I did not enter a woman's womb but I was taken into a room. There I remained conscious at all times. One day I heard the noise of little children so I thought I would go outside. Then it seemed to me that I was going through a door but I was really being born again from a woman's womb. As I walked out I was struck by a sudden gust of cold air and I began to cry.

At the place where I was brought up I was taught to fast a great deal. Afterwards I did nothing but go to war and I certainly took my revenge for my own death and that of my relatives, thus justifying the purpose for which I had come to this earth again.

There I lived until I died of old age. All at once my bones became unjointed, my ribs fell in and I died a second time. I felt no more pain at death then that I had felt the first time.

This time I was buried in the manner used then. I was wrapped in a blanket and laid in the grave. Sticks were placed in the grave first. There I rotted. I watched the people as they buried me.

As I was lying there some one said to me, "Come, let us go away." So then we went toward the land of the setting sun. There we came to a village where we met all the dead. I was told that I would have to stop there for four nights, but, in reality, I stayed there four years. The people enjoy themselves here. They have all sorts of

[6]

dances of a lively kind. From that place we went up to where Earthmaker lives and I saw him and talked to him, face to face, even as I am talking to you now. I saw the spirits too and, indeed, I was like one of them.

Thence I came to this earth for the third time and here I am. I am going through the same that I knew before.

Thus my brother-in-law had lived long ago, had joined the Medicine Dance [6] and adhered strictly to its precepts. He was a good man; he disliked no one; he never stole and never did he fight. He made offerings of tobacco to the spirits and was always giving feasts. He could always be relied upon.

When Thunder Cloud was in spirit land, just before he was to come to this earth, he fasted. He only ate once a month. All the different spirits who live on high, all those who live under the earth, indeed all those whom Earthmaker had created, they all blessed him. Then he came to the earth and was born here as a human being again. When he came to the earth he fasted. All the various spirits who had blessed him before, now blessed him again. Thus did he become a holy man. When he came here, he became a shaman for he was very holy. Indeed he was the North Spirit.

[6] The Medicine Dance is a secret society which with the preliminary ceremonies lasts five days. Members of this society are supposed to possess the secret of being able to kill one another and then to restore one another to life again. The "killing" is done by "shooting" a shell from a pouch made out of an otter skin. The shell is supposed to enter the body of the person shot at and to render him unconscious. He regains consciousness gradually after spitting out the shell. The ceremony is described in detail on pp. 103 ff. of this autobiography.

Once when I was sick he treated me. As soon as he came my father arose with tobacco in his hands and made him an offering, greeting him as follows:

"My son-in-law, tobacco do I offer you and I make offerings to your spirits. You have made your hat [7] become holy, for the various spirits made it sacred. I greet you."

Before treating me Thunder Cloud told of his fasting experience:

At the very beginning those above taught me the following. All the various spirits who live up above in the clouds, in a doctor's village, came after me and instructed me in what I was to do. They taught me and told me the following. "Here let us try it," they said to me. There in the middle of the lodge lay a rotten log, almost entirely covered with weeds. They tried to make me treat this log. I breathed upon it and all those who were in this spirit lodge also breathed upon it. Then for the second time I breathed upon it and they with me. Then for the third and the fourth time I did it. After the fourth time the rotten log arose and walked away. Then the spirits said to me, "Human being, very holy indeed are you."

There from the middle of the ocean, from the shaman's village, they came after me. They blessed me, all the spirits in the middle of the ocean. They made me try my power. As many waves as exist, all of them as large as the ocean, upon these they asked me to blow; and as I blew upon them everything became as quiet as the water in a small saucer. So they became. Then I blew for the

[7] Symbolical expression for the various objects and blessings bestowed upon him by the spirits.

[8]

third time and it was the same. The fourth time the spirits made the ocean very choppy and the waves were piled, one upon the other. Then they told me to blow again and show my power. I blew, and the ocean, mighty indeed as it was, became very quiet again. "Now this, human being, is what you will have to do," they said to me. "Not anything will there be that you cannot accomplish. Whatever be the illness a person may have, you will be able to cure him."

All the spirits on the earth blessed me. "If any human being who is suffering from pain, makes an offering of tobacco to you, then whatever you demand, that we will do for you," the spirits told me.

Now at Blue Clay Bank (St. Paul) there lives one who is a dancing grizzly-bear spirit. Whenever I am in great trouble I was to pour tobacco, as much as I thought necessary, and he would help me. This grizzly bear gave me songs and the power of beholding a holy thing; he gave me his claws, claws that are holy. Then the grizzly bear danced and performed while he danced. He tore his abdomen open and, making himself holy, healed himself again. This he repeated. One grizzly bear shot claws at the other and the wounded one became badly choked with blood. Then both made themselves holy again and cured themselves. They had a front paw disappear in the earth and after a while pulled out a prairie turnip. Finally they grabbed hold of a small plum tree, breathed upon it and shook it, and many plums began to fall.

This was only the first part of the treatment.

After recounting his fasting experience Thunder Cloud addressed the spirits and said, "Spirits, here is a person who is sick and who offers tobacco to me. I am on earth to accept it; to try and cure him." He then turned to me and said, "You will live, so help yourself as much as you can. Try to make yourself strong. Now as I offer this tobacco to the spirits you must listen and if you know that I am telling the truth, you will be strengthened thereby."

Then he prayed to the spirits:

The Prayers to the Spirits

Here, O Fire, is the tobacco for you. You promised that if I offered you some, you would grant me whatever request I made. Now I am placing tobacco on your head as you told me to do when I fasted for four days and you blessed me. I am sending you the plea of a human being who is ill. He wishes to live. This tobacco is for you and I pray that the one who is ill be restored to health within four days.

To you too, O Buffalo, I offer tobacco. A person is ill and is offering tobacco to you and asking you to restore him to health. So add that power which I obtained from you at the time I fasted for six days and you sent your spirits after me. They took me to your lodge which lies in the center of the earth and which is absolutely white. There you blessed me, you Buffaloes of four different colors. Those blessings that you bestowed upon me then, I am now in need of. The power of breathing with which you blessed me, I am now in need of. Add your power to mine as you promised.

To you, Grizzly Bear, I also offer tobacco. At a place called Pointed Hill there lives a spirit who is in charge of a ceremonial lodge, and to this all the other grizzly bears

[10]

belong. You all blessed me and you said that I would be able to kill whomsoever I wished and that I would be able to restore any person to life. Now I have a chance to enable a person to live and I wish to aid him. So here is some tobacco for you. You took my spirit to your home after I had fasted for ten days and you blessed me there. The powers with which you blessed me there I ask of you now. Here is some tobacco that the people are offering you, grandfathers.

To you, O Chief of the Eels, you who live in the center of the ocean, I offer tobacco. You blessed me after I had fasted for eight days. With your power of breathing and with your inexhaustible supply of water, you blessed me. You told me that I could use my blessing whenever I tried to cure a patient; you told me that I could use the water of the ocean and you blessed me with all the things that are in the water. A person has come to me and asked me for life. As I wish him to live I am addressing you. When I spit upon the patient may the power of my saliva be the same as yours. Therefore do I offer you tobacco. Here it is.

To you, O Turtle, you who are in charge of a shaman's lodge, you who blessed me after I had fasted for seven days, you who carried my spirit to your home, to the home of birds of prey, to you I offer tobacco. You blessed me and you told me that should, at any time, human beings suffer from pain I would be able to drive it out of them. You gave me the name of *He-who-drives-out-pain*. Now I have before me a patient with a bad pain and I wish to drive it out of him. This the spirit told me I would have the power to do, when they blessed me before I was reborn. Here is tobacco.

To you, O Rattlesnake, you who are perfectly white,

you who are in charge of the snake lodge, to you I pray. You blessed me with rattles to wrap around my gourd; you told me after I had fasted for four days that you would help me. You said that I would never fail in anything I attempted. So now when I offer you tobacco and shake my gourd, may my patient live and may life be opened out before him. That is what you promised to me, grandfather.

O Night Spirits, you also, I greet. You blessed me after I had fasted for nine days. You took my spirit to your village lying in the east, and there you gave me your flutes. You told me they were holy. My flute likewise you made holy. For your flutes I now ask you, since you know that I am speaking the truth. A sick person has come to me and has asked me to cure him. I want him to live and so I am speaking to you. You promised to accept my tobacco at all times. Here it is.

To you, too, O Disease-Giver, I offer tobacco. After I had fasted for two days you informed me that you were the one who gave disease; that if I desired to heal any one it would be easy to do so if I were blessed by you. So, Disease-Giver, I am offering tobacco to you and I ask that this sick person who has come to me, be restored to health again.

To you, O Sun, I offer tobacco. Here it is. You blessed me after I had fasted for five days and you told me you would come to my aid whenever I had something difficult to do. Now, some one is here who has pleaded for life. He has brought good offerings of tobacco to me, because he knows that you have blessed me.

To you, grandmother Earth, I also offer tobacco. You blessed me and promised to help me whenever I needed you. You said that I could use all the best herbs that grow upon you, and that I would always be able to effect cures with them. I beseech you for those herbs now and I ask you to help me to cure this sick man.

Then Thunder Cloud breathed upon me and squirted some water on my chest. "What I have said is very true and very holy, I believe," he said. "Indeed now you will get well."

Thunder Cloud knew all the good medicines that exist and he used them in order to heal me and so that I might recover from my illness. I got well. Indeed Thunder Cloud was holy.

Thunder Cloud was also what we call a poisoner. He used to travel at dead of night, it was said. One night at about eleven o'clock he got ready to poison a family by the name of B. We were all listening, sitting in our lodge. Then outside we heard him make some noise. We were afraid of him because we knew he was a poisoner. Indeed he claimed to be in control of our household. My family would do nothing without first consulting him, for we were afraid of him. We believed that he had come from the spirits, that he was a reincarnated man and, if displeased, would poison us. So whatever he asked we did.

He had been married to my eldest sister and after her death wished to marry the second sister. Where he had come from at the dwelling-place of Earth-maker,[8] my elder sister was now staying, he said. But now he claimed that the second sister resembled the

---

[8] Circumlocution for saying that she was dead.

first. "She must be the one I left behind when I came from my spirit home," he thought. So up above, to Earthmaker's village, he went to see whether his first wife was still there. He found her there. "How is this? I thought I saw you among the human beings and that is why I have come to see if you were still here," he said. And the woman answering said, "Why, where was I to go? Here you left me when you went away and here I have remained up to the present time. What kind of woman is she who resembles me? Bring her up here to me." Thus my dead sister spoke.

However since he was a bad shaman, a poisoner, we let him marry the second sister. We were afraid that if we didn't he would poison us.

He told my brother that he had come from the place where Earthmaker [9] lives, that Earthmaker had told him that he was to bring back with him four men. He was to examine them carefully, for they were to be virtuous men, not quick tempered nor of changeable ideas, but really virtuous, men of conservative tendencies. Such was he to take back with him.

My brother loved Thunder Cloud for these reasons. Never did he show any disrespect to him. Whatever he was asked to do he did. Zealously and painstakingly did he perform all the actions demanded, for he hoped that if, in return, our brother-in-law loved him and blessed him, he would take him back to Earthmaker. Wholeheartedly did he wish to be like him. This was always in his mind and he served him to the best of

[9] Earthmaker is the supreme deity of the Winnebago.

his abilities. My brother wished to return with him to Earthmaker and since he saw Thunder Cloud very scrupulous in his attitude toward Earthmaker he acted accordingly.

§3. Fasting

At this stage of life I secretly got the desire to make myself pleasing to the opposite sex.

The Indians then lived in their old-fashioned lodges. Women, however, whenever they had their menses, were placed in special huts. There the young men would go to court them at night when their parents were asleep. I used to go along with the men on such occasions, for even although I did not enter any lodges but merely accompanied the older men, I enjoyed it.

My parents were greatly in fear of my coming into contact with menstruating women so therefore I went with these men secretly. My parents were even afraid of having me cross the path over which a menstruating woman had passed. They worried so much about it at that time, because I was to fast as soon as autumn came. They did not wish me to be near menstruating women, for were I to grow up in their midst I would assuredly be weak and of little account. Such was their reason.

Before long I started to fast again together with an older brother of mine, both day and night. It was during the fall moving, and several lodges of people were living near us. There it was that my elder brother and I fasted. Among the people of the other lodges were four girls whose duty it was to carry wood.

[16]

Fasting

Whenever these girls went out to get wood my older brother and I would play around with them a great deal. We did this even although we were fasting at the time. Of course we had to do it in secret. Whenever our parents found out we got a scolding and so did the girls. At home we were warned to keep away from menstruating women, but we ourselves always sought them.

After a while some of the people living in the lodges moved away and we were left alone. They moved far ahead of us. We ourselves were to move only a short distance at a time. My father and my brother-in-law went out hunting and killed seventy deer between them, so that we had plenty of meat.

When the girls with whom I used to play moved away I became very lonesome. In the evenings I used to cry. I longed for them greatly and they had moved far away!

Soon we got fairly well started on our way back. We moved to a place where all the leaders used to give their feasts. Near the place where we lived there were three lakes and a black-hawk's nest. Right near the tree where the nest was located, they built a lodge and our war-bundle [10] was placed in it. There my elder

[10]The war-bundle was the most sacred object among the Winnebago. It consisted of dried animal skins, other parts of animals, reed flutes, etc., all of which had some symbolical meaning. The various animal remains, for instance, were supposed to give the owner the powers of these animals, the sound of the reed flutes was supposed to paralyze his enemy and make it impossible for him to walk. Each clan possessed at least one such bundle and whenever the tribe went on the warpath, this bundle was carried on the back of some

brother and myself were to pass the night. It was said that if any one fasted at such a place for four nights, he would be blessed with victory and the power to cure the sick. All the spirits would bless him.

We were told the following would happen to us. On the first night we would imagine ourselves surrounded by spirits whose whisperings we would hear outside of the lodge. The spirits would even whistle. I was told that I would be frightened and nervous and that if I still remained there, I would be molested by large monsters, fearful to look upon. Even the bravest man might well be frightened. Should I, however, manage to get through that night I would then on the following night be molested by ghosts whom I would hear speaking outside. These ghosts would say things that might well cause me to run away. Towards morning I was told these ghosts would even take my blanket away from me. They would grab hold of me and drive me out of the lodge and not stop until the sun rose. If I was able to endure a third night, then I would be addressed by the true spirits. They would bless me and say, "We bless you. We had really intended to turn you over to the monsters and bad spirits and that is why these approached you first, but you overcame them and now they will not be able to take you away. Now you may go home for we bless you with victory

individual esteemed for his bravery. The power of this war-bundle was such that it would kill anything or anybody who approached it, the only exception being a menstruating woman. For this reason the war-bundle was always carefully guarded and protected and women were not allowed to see it or come anywhere near it.

and long life; we bless you with the power of healing the sick. Nor shall you lack wealth. So go home and eat, for a large war-party is soon to fall upon you. As soon as the sun rises the war whoops will be given so that if you do not go home now you will be killed."

Thus the spirits would speak to me. I was told that if I did not care to do the bidding of one particular spirit, then some other would address me and repeat very much the same thing. So the spirits would speak alternately until the break of day. Then, just before sunrise, a man wearing a warrior's costume, would come and peep into the lodge. He would be a scout. I was told that when this happened, then I would surely believe that a war-party had come upon me. Soon another spirit would come and say, "Grandson, I have taken pity upon you and I will bless you with all the good things that the earth holds. Go home now for a war-party is about to rush upon you." If then I went home the war-whoops would be given just as the sun rose. The members of this war party would give the whoop all at the same time. They would rush upon me and capture me and after *coup* had been counted upon me (*i.e.*, after I had been struck) they would say, "Now, grandson, we have acted thus in order to teach you. Thus shall you act. You have completed your fasting."

Thus would the spirits talk to me, I was told. Now this war-party was really composed of spirits, spirits from the heaven and the earth. Indeed all the spirits that exist would be there. These would all bless me.

[19]

I was also told that it would be a very difficult thing to obtain this particular blessing.

So there I fasted at the black-hawk's nest, where a lodge had been built for me. The first night I stayed there I wondered when something would happen. But nothing took place. The second night, rather late in the night, my father came and opened the war-bundle and then taking out a gourd, began to sing. I stood beside him without any clothing except my breech-clout and, holding tobacco in each hand, I uttered my cry to the spirits:

"O spirits, here humble in heart I stand beseeching you."

My father sang war-bundle songs and wept as he sang. I also wept as I uttered my cry to the spirits. When he was finished he told me some sacred stories; he told me about my ancestor Weshgishega:

The Story of My Ancestor Weshgishega

When Weshgishega was growing up his father coaxed him to fast. He told him that when Earthmaker had created the various spirits, all the good ones he had created, were placed in charge of something. The gift of bestowing upon man life and victory in war he gave to some; to others, the gift of hunting-powers. Whatever powers the Indians needed in order to live, these he placed in the hands of various spirits. These blessings Weshgishega's father told Weshgishega to attempt to obtain from the spirits.

Thus Weshgishega fasted and tried to obtain something

[20]

from the spirits. But as he fasted he kept thinking to himself, "Long ago Earthmaker created all the different spirits and he put every one of them in control of something, so people say. He himself must therefore be much more powerful than all the others. As holy as these spirits are, so assuredly, Earthmaker must be mightier, holier." So he thought. He tried to be blessed by Earthmaker. He thought to himself, "What kind of being is he?" As he fasted Weshgishega thought to himself, "Not even any of the spirits whom Earthmaker created has really known Earthmaker as he actually is; not one of the spirits has he even blessed. I wonder, however, whether Earthmaker would bless me? This is what I am thinking of." So he put himself into a most pitiable condition and uttered his cry to the spirits. He could not stop. "From Earthmaker do I wish to obtain knowledge. If he does not bless me during my fasting I shall assuredly die." So, to the utmost of his power, did he fast. He wished to be blessed only by Earthmaker.

At first he fasted four days; then six; then eight; then ten and finally twelve days. After that he broke his fast. Yet it was quite clear that he had obtained no knowledge, quite clear that he had not been blessed. So he gave up his fasting and when he reached the age of early manhood he married.

He took his wife, and the two of them moved to an out-of-the-way place. There they lived, he and his wife.

Here again he commenced to fast, his wife with him. He wished to be blessed by Earthmaker. This time he felt that most assuredly would he die if Earthmaker did not appear before him in his fasting. "Never has it been told that such a thing could happen, that Earthmaker would bless any one. Yet I shall continue even if I have to die."

After a while a child was born to him. It was a boy. He addressed his wife and asked her advice, saying that they ought to sacrifice their child to Earthmaker. She consented. To Earthmaker therefore they prepared to sacrifice their child. They constructed a platform and placed their child upon it.[11] Then both of them wept bitterly. In the nighttime when the man slept, Earthmaker took pity on him and appeared to him. The man looked at him. He thought, "This, most certainly, is Earthmaker." He wore a soldier's uniform and carried a high cocked hat on his head. He had a very pleasing appearance. Weshgishega looked at him and wondered whether this really was Earthmaker. The figure took one step, then another, and finally disappeared, uttering a cry. It was not Earthmaker; it was a pigeon. The bad spirits were fooling Weshgishega.

Now even more than before did his heart ache, even more than before was his heart wound up in the desire to be blessed by Earthmaker. Now again he fasted and again apparently Earthmaker appeared to him. "Human being, I bless you. Long have you made your cry for a blessing. I am Earthmaker." When Weshgishega looked at him, he saw that he was pleasing in appearance. He looked very handsome and his dress was nice to look upon. He wondered whether this really was Earthmaker. As he looked at the figure it became smaller and smaller and when finally he looked, he noticed that it was a bird.

Then his heart ached even more than before. Bitterly did he cry. Now, for the third time, Earthmaker blessed him saying, "Human being, you have tried to be blessed by Earthmaker and you have caused yourself great suf-

[11] That is, they killed the child and then placed his body upon a platform, this being the customary mode of burial of the clan to which Weshgishega belonged.

fering. I am Earthmaker and I bless you. You will never be in want of anything; you will be able to understand the languages of your neighbors; you will have a long life; indeed, with everything do I bless you." But, from the very first, this figure did not inspire Weshgishega with confidence and he thought to himself, "Somebody must be fooling me." And so it was; it was a bird.

Then most assuredly did he think that he wished to die for he felt that all the bad birds in the world were trying to make fun of him.

Earthmaker, above where he sits, knew of all this. He heard the man's voice and he said, "O Weshgishega, you are crying. I shall come to the earth for you. Your father has told me all." Then when Weshgishega looked, he saw a ray of light extending very distinctly from the sky down to the earth. To the camp it extended. "Weshgishega, you said that you wanted to see me. That, however, cannot be. But I am the ray of light. You have seen me."

Not with any war powers did Earthmaker bless him; only with life.

After telling me about Weshgishega, father left me. When I found myself alone I began to think that something ought to happen soon, yet nothing occurred so I had to pass another day there. On the third night I was still there. My father visited me again and we repeated what we had done on the night before. He told me about my grandfather Jobenangiwinxga:

My Ancestor Jobenangiwinxga

Once Jobenangiwinxga fasted. So that he might be blessed by the spirits he starved and thirsted himself to death; he made himself pitiable in their sight. At first he fasted four nights and the Night Spirits came to him; with mighty sounds they came. There they stood before him and said, "Human being, you have thirsted yourself to death and we are going to bless you for that reason. We who speak are the Night Spirits." They blessed him with life and with success on the warpath. Then he looked at them and said to himself, "I wonder whether these really are the Night Spirits speaking to me?" Then he looked at them and he saw that they were small birds called heshepga. They had fooled him.

Then once again was his heart sore. In despair he said, "Well, if I have to, I'll die fasting." So he fasted again and once again he rubbed charcoal on his face. For six nights he continued to fast. And then, once again, from the east the Night Spirits came. They came making a great noise and they stood near him and said, "Human being, we bless you. You have thirsted yourself to death and you have made your heart sore. We feel sad on your account. With life and success on the warpath we bless you." Then he looked at them and again he wondered in his heart whether they really were the Night Spirits.[12] Indeed they were not the Night Spirits who were speaking to him. They were birds called the kawishge, choxjin and shikokkok. They were fooling him. Instead of feeling sad this time, however, he said, "I don't care what happens; I am willing to die in order to get a blessing." So he thought to himself.

Then again he began fasting. He rubbed charcoal over

[12] The Night Spirits were mythical spirits whose precise nature is never described in detail. They are supposed to cause darkness and the night. They possess a cane with which they strike those of their worshipers who are not properly attentive to their ceremonies.

Fasting

his face again. Seven nights he fasted and once again from the east the Night Spirits came singing. They came and stood before him and said, "Nephew, we bless you. So long have you been sad and so piteously have you cried to us that we bless you. No one did we ever bless before. Both in war and in life you shall be able to do as you wish." Then again he looked in their direction and thought to himself, "I wonder whether those speaking are really the Night Spirits?" But indeed they were not the Night Spirits They were the bluebird and the duck and as many as there were of them, their breasts were dark; as many as there were of them, they were bad. "O my! O my! How they abuse me," Jobenangiwinxga cried.

He had at first thought in his fastings that just to spite the spirits he would fast again but now he rubbed charcoal on his face and wept bitterly. Both hands contained tobacco, and he stood in the direction from which the Night Spirits came and, weeping, put himself in the most abject condition.

Now indeed to its very depths did his heart ache. Ten nights did he fast. Finally the Night Spirits came after him. "Human being, I have come after you." He followed the spirits and they took him to the east; to the site of a Night Spirit village they took him. In the village there was a long lodge standing in the east. There they took him. All the Night Spirits in control of the most powerful blessings were there. When he entered he had to wade through white feathers up to his knees. Many kettles and much food did he see in the lodge. On the outside a buffalo hide was stretched almost across the entire lodge. Then these spirits said to him, "Human being, without giving up, long have you suffered; your heart has indeed been sad. All of the spirits in this lodge have talked about what is to happen to you. I, myself, am the chief of the Night Spirits. This creation lodge, just as you see it, with all that it contains, I give to you. Never shall you be in want of food. Offer up to us as many buckskins as you see here in the lodge. Thus it shall be. The creation lodge of the village of the Night Spirits I give to you. You can go on as many war-parties as you wish and you will obtain everything that you demand of life. All the offerings of tobacco, of food, of buckskins, and of red feathers, that you and your descendants offer to us, they all will come here to our creation lodge and we will accept them."

Now thus did the Night Spirits speak to grandfather Jobenangiwinxga.

In the morning, just before sunrise, I uttered my cry to the spirits:

"O spirits, here humble in heart I stand beseeching you."

The fourth night found me still there. Again my father came and we did the same thing, but in spite of it all I experienced nothing unusual. Soon another day dawned upon us. That morning I told my elder brother that I had been blessed by the spirits and that I was going home to eat. I was not speaking the truth. I was hungry and I also knew that on the following night we were going to have a feast, and that we would have to utter our cry to the spirits again. I dreaded that. So I went home. When I got there I told my people the story I had told my brother; that I had been blessed and that the spirits had told me to eat. I was not speaking the truth, yet I was given the food that is carefully prepared for those who have been blessed.

Fasting

Just then my older brother came home and they objected to his return for he had not been blessed. However, he took some food and ate it.

My brother J., however, obtained a blessing. When he reached the age of puberty my father called him aside and told him to fast. He told him that it was his fervent wish that he should begin to fast in order to become holy, to become invincible and invulnerable in war. He wished him to become like one of those Winnebago of whom stories are told. He assured him that if he fasted he would really be holy and that nothing that exists on this earth would be able to molest him; that he would live a very long life and that he would be able to cure the sick. He told him that if he were blessed no one would dare to make fun of him and that they would be very careful how they addressed him; first, because they really respected him and secondly, because they were afraid of getting him angry. He was to fast until spring and then he was to stop, for there are many bad spirits about in the spring who are likely to deceive a faster.

Near our village there was a hill called *Place-where-they-keep-weapons*. This hill was very high, steep and rocky. It was a very holy place. There it was that my father wished my brother to fast for it was the place where he himself had fasted. Within this hill lived the spirits whom we call *Those-who-cry-like-babies*. These spirits are supposed to possess arrows and bows. Twenty of them were supposed to be in this hill. My father had control of them and when he wished to bless a man he would take his bow and arrows and, holding them in his hands, lead the man around the hill and into the lodge (*i.e.,* into the hill). There he would look for a stone pillar, and upon it, at about arm's length, he drew the pictures of a number of different animals. My father possessed only one arrow, but that one was a holy one. Then dancing around the stone pillar and singing some songs, he finished by breathing upon the pillar. Finally he walked around and shot at it and when he looked at the stone, it had turned into a deer with large horns which fell dead at his feet. He repeated this a number of times. The little spirits living in the hill breathed with him and said, "Winnebago, whenever you wish to kill a deer with one horn, do as you have done, and offer us tobacco and you will be able to obtain whatever you wish."

This was the power my father wished my brother to obtain. My father was a very famous hunter and my brother wished to be like him.

Now of all these things my brother dreamed; with all these powers he was blessed. He also had a vision of visiting the village of the ghosts. There he was able to steal a costly shawl and escape with it. He dreamed that all the inhabitants of the ghost village chased him but that they were unable to overtake him and were compelled to return back when my brother reached the earth.

The night after we had stopped fasting we gave our feast. There, however, our pride received a fall, for although the feast was supposedly given in our honor, we were placed on one side of the main participants. After the kettles containing the food had been put on twice, it became daylight and the feast was over.

The following spring we moved to the Mississippi in order to trap. I was still fasting and ate only at night. My brothers used to flatter me, telling me that I was the cleverest of them all and, in consequence, I used to continue fasting although I was often very hungry. In spite of my desire to fast, however, I could not resist the temptation of being around the girls. I wanted always to be near them. They were generally in their menstrual lodges [13] when I looked for them. My parents did not wish me to go near the girls then but I went nevertheless.

My parents told me that only those boys who had no connection with women would be blessed by the spirits. Throughout this time my sole wish was to appear great in the sight of the people. To be praised by my fellowmen was all I desired. And I certainly received what I sought. I stood high in their estima tion. That the women might like me was another of the reasons why I wanted to fast. But as to being blessed, I learned nothing about it, although I went around with the air of one who had received many blessings and talked as such a one would talk.

[13] Any contact with menstruating women, or even with objects in any way connected with them, will, it is the firm belief of the Winnebago, destroy the power of sacred objects or individuals temporarily sacred. Fasting youths were regarded as such.

§4. *Reminiscences of Childhood*

The following spring I stopped fasting.

In those days we used to travel in canoes. My father used to spear fish and always took me along with him, and this I enjoyed very much. He kept a club in the canoe and after he had speared a fish, I would kill it with the club as it was jumping around. Sometimes my mother accompanied us. She sat in the stern of the boat and rowed while my father stood in the prow and speared the fish. I killed all those thrown in the canoe.

Sometimes my parents would start out without me, but I would then cry so bitterly that I, in the long run, induced them to take me along. Sometimes they whipped me and told me to go home, but I would follow them so far that they were then afraid to let me go back alone and I would thus be permitted to ride with them. Indeed I exerted myself greatly in crying and as I cried, ran after them and followed them very far, I was always taken along in the end.

In those days we lived in the old-fashioned Indian lodges. In winter our fire was placed in the center of the lodge and my father used to keep it burning all night. When he placed a large log in the fire it would burn a long time.

Reminiscences of Childhood

We were three boys of whom I was the youngest and at night we slept together. In cold weather we fought as to who was to sleep in the middle, since whoever got that place was warm; for while those at either end used to pull the cover from each other, the one in the middle was always covered. Even after I grew up I always took the cover away from the particular person with whom I happened to be sleeping. I would always fold it under me, for it had become a habit with me to take the cover away from the other person whenever I slept on the outside.

We always ate out of one dish. At times we did not have enough food on hand and then I would always try to get enough by eating very fast. In this way I often succeeded in depriving the others of their proper portion. Sometimes, on the other hand, I would purposely eat slowly and then when the others were finished, I would say that I had not been given enough and so get some of their food. In this way I developed a habit, that I still have, of eating fast. Even after I grew up, whenever I ate with other people, I always finished sooner than they did.

Another habit acquired then was the ability to go without food for a whole day while traveling. I did not mind this in the least, for during my fasting I had grown accustomed to going without food for long periods of time.

In the summer, at the season when people pick berries, I used to go around visting, sometimes for a day, sometimes for a longer period. I would often receive nothing to eat, but I did not mind that. In the summer, when people pick berries, they generally go out in bands and settle here and there. Some would be living at a great distance from the others.

§5. Names

Whenever they think highly of any individual in a family they give him the means for obtaining a happy life. If the older people think highly of any one they prearrange the kind of life he is to lead afterwards. With this object in view, my uncles told my brother the story of how human beings first came into this world, the story of the origin of our clan.

The Story of the Origin of Our Clan

Earthmaker was sitting in space when he came to consciousness. Nothing was to be found anywhere. He began to think of what he was to do and finally he cried. Tears flowed from his eyes and fell below where he was sitting. After a while he looked below and saw something bright. The bright objects were tears, of which he had not been aware and, which falling below, had formed the present waters. They became the seas of to-day. Then Earthmaker began to think again. He thought, "Thus it is whenever I wish anything. Everything will become as I wish it just as my tears have become the water of the seas." So he wished for light and it became light. Then he thought, "It is as I have supposed; the things that I wished for, come into existence as I desired." Then he again thought and wished for this earth and this earth came into existence. Earthmaker looked at the earth and he liked it, but it was not quiet. It moved about as do the waves of the seas. Then he made the trees and he saw that they were good. But even these did not make the earth quiet. Then he made the grass grow and still the earth was not quiet. It was however almost quiet. Then he created the four cardinal points and the four winds. At the four corners of the earth he placed them as four great and powerful spirits, to act as weights holding down this island earth of ours. Yet still the earth was not quiet. Then he made four large beings and threw them down toward the earth and they were pierced through the earth with their heads eastward. They were really snake-beings. Then it was that the earth became still and quiet. Now he looked upon the earth and he liked it.

Again he thought of how things came into existence just as he desired. Then it was that he first spoke and said, "As everything happens just as I wish it, I shall make a man like myself in appearance." So he took a piece of earth and made it like himself. Then he talked to what he had created but it did not answer. He looked at it and he saw that it had no mind or thought. So he made a mind for it. Again he talked to it but it did not answer. So he looked at it again and he saw that it had no tongue. Then he made it a tongue. Then he talked to it again but it did not answer. So he looked at it and he saw that it had no soul. So he made it a soul. He talked to it again and then it very nearly said something but could not make itself intelligible. So Earthmaker breathed into its mouth and talked to it and it answered.

As the newly created being was very much like Earthmaker in appearance, he felt quite proud of him, so he made three more exactly similar. He made them powerful so that they might watch over the earth. These four he

[34]

made chiefs of the Thunderbirds. Then he thought, "I will have some beings live on the earth." So he made four more like himself. Just like the others he made them. They were brothers—*Kunuga, Henuga, Hagaga* and *Nangiga.* He talked to them and said, "Look down upon the earth.' So saying he opened the heavens in the place where they were standing and there they saw this earth spread out before them. He told them that they were to go down there to live. "And this I shall send down with you," he added giving them a plant. "Even I shall never have the power of taking this away from you, for I have given it to you exclusively; but when, of your own free will, you make me an offering of some of it, I shall be glad to accept it and give you in return whatever you ask. This shall you hold foremost in your lives." What he had given them was the tobacco-plant. Then again he spoke and said, "All the spirits that I have created will not be able to take this away from you unless you desire to give it to them, by calling upon them during fasts. Thus only can the spirits get some. And another thing I send with you that you may use it in life, to be a mediator between you and us, whenever you offer anything to the spirits. It shall take care of you throughout life, stand in the center of your dwellings, and be your grandfather." This was the Fire.

Then the four Thunderbirds brought the brothers down to the earth. On their journey down *Kunuga,* the oldest of the four, said, "Brother, when we get to earth and the first child is born to me, I shall call him *Chief-of-the-Thunderbirds,* if he is a boy." On and on they came, down toward the earth. As they got near the earth it began to get very dark and then the second brother said, "Brother, when we get to the earth and a child is born to me, if it is a girl, I shall call her *Dark.*" Then they came to a place called

Within-lake at Red Banks, a lake near Green Bay (Wisconsin). On an oak tree south of the lake is the place where they alighted. The branch on which they alighted was bent down by their weight. Then spoke the third brother, "Brother, the first daughter born to me I shall call *She-who-weighs-the-tree-down.*" Then they alighted on the earth. Then said the fourth brother, "Brother, the first son born to me I shall call *He-who-alights-on-the-earth.*" Then the brothers alighted on the earth. But the thunderbirds did not touch the earth. The first thing the brothers did on earth was to start fire.

Then Earthmaker looked down upon them and saw that he had not prepared any food, so he created animals that they might have something to eat. The oldest brother suddenly said, "What are we going to eat?" Thereupon the youngest two took a bow and arrow Earthmaker had given them and started toward the east. Shortly after, the third brother came into sight with a young deer on his back and then the youngest appeared with a two years' old deer. The two deer killed and those who had killed them, were brothers.

The men were very much delighted that they had obtained food. Then they said, "Let us give our grandfather the first taste." So saying they cut off the ends of the tongues, cut out the heart and together with some fat, threw both into the fire.

The first people to call on them were the Warrior clan people. Then came those from the west, four of them, the Pigeon clan people. Then came those of the earth, the Deer people, the Snake people, the Elk people, the Bear people, the Fish people, the Waterspirit people and all the other clans that exist among the Winnebago.

Names

Finally there appeared on the lake a very white bird, the swan. After that all the other birds in the world appeared. They were named in the order of their coming until the lake was quite full. Then the people began to dress the deer meat. Suddenly something came and alighted on the meat and one of the brothers asked, "What is that?" Then said *Kunuga* the eldest, "It is a wasp and the first black dog that I possess, I shall call *Wasp*." "Just as the wasp scented and became aware of the deer meat as it was being dressed, so shall the dog be toward other animals. Whenever an animal is on the windward the dog will scent it," *Kunuga* continued.

Then they made a feast for Earthmaker with the deer meat, threw tobacco into the fire and gave some to him. They showed the other clans how to make fire and gave a little to each adding, "Each of you must now learn how to make fire for yourselves for we shall not always lend you some." Here then it was that the first people who lived made their homes. They had come at the time of the year when the grass grows as far as the knee.

One day it was reported that a very strange object was nearing the camp. The men thought at first that they would leave it alone. It came nearer and nearer and as it moved toward the camp it began to eat the bones it found there. They allowed this animal to become the founder of one of their clans and took it to their homes. It was the dog. Then they killed one of these dogs and offered it up to Earthmaker telling him all they had done.

In the beginning the Thunderbird clansmen were as powerful as the Thunderbird spirits themselves. It was they who made the ravines and the valleys. While wandering about the earth they struck the earth with their clubs and

[37]

thus created dents in the hills. That is why the Thunder-bird clansmen are the chiefs. The Dog-clan people are the least in importance.

One day the oldest of the brothers lay down and did not rise again. He did not breathe and his body became cold. "What is the matter with our oldest brother?" the other three said. Four days they waited for him but he did not get up. They tried to find out from one another what the trouble was but did not succeed. Then they began to mourn for him not knowing what to do or think. They fasted and blackened their faces as we do now when we are mourning. They made a burial platform and placed him upon it. When the snow fell and it was knee-deep then, filling their pipe, the three brothers walked in the direction of the coming of daylight. They came to the first spirit Earthmaker had placed in the east, the *Island Weight* as he was called. Weeping they entered his lodge and extended the stem of their pipe toward him and spoke, "Grandfather, our brother *Kunuga* has fallen down and is not able to rise again. Earthmaker made you great and endowed you with all knowledge so that you know all things. Tell us what has happened to our brother?" Then he answered, "My grandsons, I am indeed sorry but I know nothing about this. Since, however, you have started on this quest you had better go to the one ahead of me, the north *Island Weight*. Perhaps he can tell you."

So weeping they started for the next one. When they got there and told him their troubles he told them he could not help and referred them to his third brother in the west. Thus in turn they were referred to the last of the *Island Weights*, the one in the south. There they found all four of the *Island Weights* assembled and the south one answered and spoke, "Grandsons, thus Earthmaker has

willed it. Your brother will never rise again. He will be
with you no more on this world and so it will be with human
beings as long as the world exists. Whenever a person
reaches the age of death, he will die. Those that wish to
live long will have to attain old age through good actions.
Thus only will they succeed in living long. Into your bodies
Earthmaker has placed a part of himself and that will return to him if you do the proper things. This world will
at sometime come to an end. Your brother is to keep a
village in the west for all the souls of your clan and there
he is going to be in complete charge. When this world
comes to an end then your brother will take all the souls
back to Earthmaker—at least all those who have acted
properly." Then the Thunderbird clansmen thanked the
four spirits and left the lodge.

When they got home they took their brother's body,
dressed him in his best clothes and painted his face. Then
they addressed the dead person and told him where he
was to go. They buried him with his war club, his head
toward the west. At the grave they placed the branch of
a tree and to this branch they tied a small red stick in
order to prevent anything from crossing his path, in his
journey to spirit-land. He was told that if any animal
crossed his path or was found on his path during the journey, he was to strike it with his club and throw it behind
him, so that those of his relatives whom he had left behind
on earth might derive blessings for the warpath, and attain long life. He must take his pipe and his food along
with him. Whatever years he was deprived of when he
died, all the victories he might have gained had he lived to
a normal old age, all these he was to bestow upon his relatives. The wealth he might have gained, in fact anything
he could possibly have obtained, all this he was asked to

give to his relatives. Then they would not feel so unhappy and lonesome.

Now in our clan whenever a child was to be named it was my father who did it. That right he now transmitted to my brother.

Earthmaker, in the beginning, sent four men from above and when they came to this earth everything that happened to them was utilized in making proper names. This is what our father told us. As they had come from above so from that fact has originated a name *Comes-from-above;* and since they came like spirits we have a name *Spirit-man.* When they came, there was a drizzling rain and hence the names *Walking-in-mist, Comes-in-mist, Drizzling-rain.* It is said that when they came to *Within-lake* they alighted upon a small shrub and hence the name *Bends-the-shrub;* and since they alighted on an oak tree, the name *Oak-tree.* Since our ancestors came with the thunderbirds we have a name *Thunderbird* and since these are the animals who cause thunder, we have the name *He-who-thunders.* Similarly we have *Walks-with-a-mighty-tread, Shakes-the-earth-down-with-his-force, Comes-with-wind-and-hail, Flashes-in-every-direction, Only-a-flash-of-lightning, Streak-of-lightning, Walks-in-the-clouds, He-who-has-long-wings, Strikes-the-tree.*

Now the thunderbirds come with terrible thundercrashes. Everything on the earth, animals, plants, everything, is deluged with rain. Terrible thundercrashes resound everywhere. From all this a name is derived and that is my name—*Crashing Thunder.*

§6. *Stories*

When we were children my father used to tell us
stories in the evening. Whenever we showed signs of
restlessness he stopped. Here are some of the stories
that I remember.

The Story of Coyote and the Ghost

Coyote was wandering about alone. He was wandering
about aimlessly looking for food; he was scenting around
everywhere for food, for he was very hungry. As he was
walking from place to place he suddenly became aware
of the scent of human flesh. "Ah! Ah! If there are any
human beings in the neighborhood surely they have thrown
away bits of food and I shall be able to get some." So
he started in the direction of the scent and soon he got to
an old abandoned village and picked up some moccasins,
but he could find nothing that would satisfy his hunger. He
wandered to the end of the village thinking, "Perhaps
here at the end of the village I may find some graves and
possibly the bodies there will still have some flesh on
them." But not even graves could he find.

In the distance, however, he saw a rack and when he
ran toward it eager to see what it was, he saw a corpse
lying on top. A man had died and his body had been
placed on a burial scaffold. "Oh my! Oh my!" he exclaimed, "if this body were only on the ground then indeed

I would have my fill." Badly did he want to eat but there was nothing that he could do. So he sat there always looking upwards at the corpse, hungry. He would at times leave it but then return again. This was in the fall of the year and as he sat there he thought, "How I wish this corpse were on the ground! It would last me till spring."

When night came on, Coyote was still there. He prepared to sleep there. Suddenly the corpse spoke, "Coyote, what do I smell like?" Coyote got frightened but he thought to himself, "What shall I say to him?" "Well, what could you possibly smell like, but like small dried corn boiled with bear's ribs." "Good," said the ghost, "come and get it." So Coyote sprang forward and there, much to his surprise, he found a big dish full of corn boiled with bear's ribs. And Coyote, the covetous fellow, ate very much.

The next morning the ghost again spoke to Coyote, "Coyote, what do I smell like?" "What indeed could you smell like, but like jerked meat in bear's fat." "Good, come and get it." And there again he found a plate full of jerked meat and bear's fat. And Coyote, the covetous fellow, ate very much.

In this way every morning and every evening he obtained food. Dried corn boiled with fruit and watermelon, these too he ate. Coyote, the covetous fellow, ate very much.

All winter he lived there with the corpse. Every morning and evening the corpse would ask the same question. One day Coyote decided to ask for something special, so he waited anxiously for the corpse to speak, "Well, Coyote, what do I smell like?" "What could you smell like, but like a bottle of whisky, of dark red color. "Good, come and get it," said the ghost. So there he went and found a square bottle. He pulled the cork out of it, took a drink and before long he was hopelessly drunk. He finished the bottle but he wanted more. Soon it was filled again. In his happiness he gave a war whoop and soon emptied it. Then he lay down drunk. The next morning he was sober, but he was sick of whisky and when the corpse spoke to him he asked for some deer-loin soup. This he drank avidly for as he became sober he was very thirsty. Four times during the winter he got drunk and four times he always sobered up in the same way.

Spring was now near at hand and he began meditating upon what he should ask for. Then as the corpse shouted over to him, "Coyote, what do I smell like?" he answered, "Well, what could you smell like but like a warpath?" "Good, Coyote, you may go on a warpath. One man you may go after; one man I bestow upon you." So Coyote started out on the warpath. He came to a village and there he dug up a grave and from it he took a scalp. With this he returned victoriously to the corpse. Before leaving he had sung his farewell song:

"Oh, you grass widows! Oh, you grass widows! When you look at your work, surely you will think of me!"

When he returned with a man's scalp he danced the victory dance, all by himself.

Spring had now come, the real spring. The weather was beautiful; the green grass was up and the days were pleasant. Coyote contemplated himself and he liked his appearance. "How splendid I look!" Sleek and fat he was. He felt like wandering around and visiting people. When, therefore in the morning, the corpse asked, "Coyote, what do I smell like?" he answered, "Well, what indeed could you smell like, but like a stinking corpse with hollow eyes?" "Oh, you greedy, covetous fellow," exclaimed the corpse, "you shall die for this!" Then he chased him but always, at the last minute, just as he was about to be caught, he managed to escape. Finally Coyote ran into a hole and the corpse stationed himself outside and said, "Coyote, you have saved yourself for the present, but surely you do not deserve to be blessed and I will not rest till I have killed you." Just then the corpse grabbed hold of Coyote's tail and the end of it broke off.

Coyote managed to escape eventually and as he ran along he sang:

"Uncles, my uncles! Uncles, my uncles! A corpse has bitten off my tail!"

A bear passed, but he could not help him. Finally, however, a deer, the kind we call chiakshigega, came along and gave him part of his tail. So Coyote had a tail the end of which was white. He liked it very much and as he ran along, he looked at it again and again. He was very proud of it.

Now this is the reason the chiakshigega deer have short tails and this is the reason why the tip of the Coyote's tail is white.

The Story of the Man Who Avenged the Death of His Wife

Once an old man lived together with his daughter and son-in-law in one lodge. He was too old to trap or hunt any longer and so depended entirely upon his son-in-law for food. Now this old man possessed the right to give the war-bundle feast and one day he told his daughter that she was to take her husband and her children and accompany him while he hunted for the deer to be used for the feast.

So the husband left with his family and went to a place

[44]

about two days' distance from their camp. They arrived at the destined place at evening and the woman pitched the tent, while the man went out to gather wood. Since there was nothing to eat he told his wife that he would go in search of food immediately. He took his bow and arrows and left. While he was gone the woman fetched some water, filled the kettle and put it on the fire so that it would be ready when her husband returned. At dusk he returned carrying a deer on his back. This he set down outside and the woman skinned it and prepared it in the usual manner by cutting it first into small pieces and then drying these by the heat of the fire. Then they all sat down and ate and, shortly after, went to bed. The woman and children were soon fast asleep but the man stayed awake planning the hunt for the following day, for he wished very much to please his father-in-law. On the following morning he told his wife that if, during his absence, anything should happen she was under no circumstances to leave the children. Then he took his bow and his arrows and went away.

Now in the olden days it was considered a very brave thing for a man to camp at some distance from the main settlement and that is why, on this occasion when he was leaving, the man said to his wife, "If anything happens to you while I am away, remember that I will return immediately." He wished to show how much he loved her. He was out all day hunting and he killed a deer, skinned it and began carrying it home on his back. When he was near the site of his little camp he noticed that the lodgepoles were all standing upright and he knew immediately what had happened; he knew at once that his wife and children had either been killed or captured. He felt terrible but he laughed when he reached the lodge and found his wife gone and the children dead. The bodies of the children had been placed in a standing posture against the door. Their lips were parted so that they might thus convey to their father on his return, the impression of smiling at him. This was an old custom and it was done because the enemy thought that, in this way, they could cause a father the most pain.

When the man returned and saw all this, he quietly attended to the fire, prepared his meal and then addressed the children saying to them, "Come, this is the last meal that we will take together." Then he pried open their mouths and put a piece of meat in their throats. After he had fed them, he himself sat down to eat. When he was through he painted his body in two colors, one side from head to foot white and the other from head to foot black. Then he again spoke to the children, "My dear children, I believe I can go on a few warpaths myself and I shall endeavor to send your spirits to the spirit land as properly as I know how. I shall kill the people who have slain you and many more to boot."

Then he put some arrows in his quiver and buried his children. Starting out he soon found himself in a trail and by carefully scrutinizing the footprints he discovered those of his wife, and thus knew that she had been taken prisoner. Now he transformed himself into a ghost and following the trail, found the enemy not far away. He ran ahead of them and waited, and as one of the enemy who was carrying the medicine pouch approached, he gave a whoop and killed him, cutting off his head as far as the neck. Then he disappeared in the brush, hid the head and ran ahead again. So he killed one after another, eight in all. When day dawned he returned to the camp with his eight heads and eight war clubs. These he first placed around his camping site, but then picking them up started for the home of his own father.

Thus, with the eight heads, he came to his father's lodge, but he did not enter it until late at night. Then when all his people were asleep, he blackened his face and entering the lodge, sat down in the place he had occupied before he had married. The old man suddenly saw some one sitting in his son's accustomed seat and awakening his wife he said to her, "There is some one sitting in our son's seat who looks exactly like our son." Both of them then sat up and soon they discovered that it really was their son and that he was in mourning, his face all blackened with charcoal.

Then the old man spoke, "My son, what is the matter?" And the son answered, "Father, a war-party came upon my camp while I was out hunting, took my wife prisoner, and killed my children." "My son, if you had any respect for yourself, why did you not die with your children?" "Father, let me explain to you how it happened. While I was out hunting they fell upon my lodge, killed my two children and took my wife prisoner. When I came back I felt very miserable but I laughed and cooked my own meal, fed the children and ate with them for the last time. Then I pursued the war party and on that very night I killed eight of them, whose heads and war clubs I have brought home with me. Near the spring I have hidden them. There I placed the heads in a row and there I planted the war clubs in the ground, one near each head." "My son," said the father, "you have done well and the souls of your children will certainly reach the spirit land safely. For us, too, you have brought some nice heads, so that we might derive some amusement from them. I am very thankful to you."

In the morning the father sent the crier around the vil-

lage with the news of what his son had accomplished all
alone. All the men in the village put on their war paint,
took their war clubs and ran to the place where the heads
had been deposited. There each man struck one and giving
the war whoop, counted *coup* on the enemy. Then they
took the heads and brought them to their war lodge. There
the victory dance was given and there all praised the man
who had accomplished this brave deed.

When the dance was over the man again blackened his
face and fasted for ten days. His people gave a feast
when he had finished his fast, and at this feast he told
them that he was now going on the warpath to rescue his
wife who had been captured, and that all those who wished
to come along could do so. "To-morrow at dawn," he
said, "we will get ready and go to a certain hill and from
there start out." So the next morning they gathered at
the appointed place and started out. The man led the
expedition. They marched all that day and toward evening they built their fires and sat around the fireplace
while the old warriors told war exploits. The next day
they marched all day again and so on until the third
day. On the fourth day the man said, "Now here I shall
attempt to locate the whereabouts of the enemy." So he
went away and on that very night he succeeded in approaching the enemy's village. He found them all asleep. Then
he went to his wife and said, "I have come to get you. The
spirit who is in charge of this war-party has given this
whole village to me and to-morrow we shall kill them all.
Your brothers are outside with me and to-morrow, when
we rush upon these people, you must run toward your
brothers and tell them that you want to be a prisoner. I
shall tell my friends to be on the lookout for you and not
kill you. Now remember, do as I tell you, for if you don't,

they will kill you!" "I shall try," said the woman. Then the man returned to his followers and told them that everything was well and cautioned them about the woman, telling the brothers also to see that she was not killed.

When day dawned they fell upon the village and surprised it. They fought nearly half a day and killed practically every one except the head chiefs and their sons, whom they took prisoners. They then returned home. When they reached the village they took both the prisoners and the captured scalps to their war lodge where they were guarded. The next morning they tied the prisoners to posts, danced around them and tortured them till they died.

Now such is the story of a man who was faithful to the spirit from whom he had received war blessings. He gave feasts and he made offerings in their honor. He fasted and his prayers were answered.

The Story of the Man Who Rescued His Wife from Spirit-land

In a certain village there once lived two young married people. The woman was very beautiful and her husband loved her very much. Always he was thinking of something that he could do for her.

One day the young woman got ill. They called for a shaman but he could do nothing for her. Many were the holy men the young husband called, but it was all of no avail and the young woman died. They buried her. On the evening of the funeral many friends came to the grave to place lights there, so that the soul of the departed might find its way through spirit land. The young man was very good and every one liked him. They all came to the Four

Nights' Wake and they all played the mourning games with him. Then on the morning after the fourth night they all went home and the young man was left alone.

Immediately he made preparations to journey toward the west, for it is said that the soul of the deceased goes in that direction. In the direction of the west did he therefore chase the soul of his wife. As he trudged along the road he became worn out with exertion and fatigue and finally found it necessary to support himself on a cane. Even for that, however, his strength was not adequate and after a while all he could do was to barely creep along. Soon his knees were worn out from the incessant crawling and he tied some basswood bark around them. Thus he continued until all his strength deserted him. He was just strong enough to crawl to a pleasant-looking knoll. "This," he said, "is pleasant and nice and here I am willing to die." He rolled over until he finally reached the coveted spot and there lay awaiting death with his eyes closed.

Suddenly, much to his surprise, he heard some one talking to him, saying, "Come let us go home. I live here." The young man opened his eyes and looked about him and there before him he saw a fearful-looking person whose body was entirely covered with hair. The young man was unable to get up but the stranger spoke to him and said, "Come on!" At this the young man jumped up and followed him around the lodge. There the old man said to him, "Grandson, you are indeed in a most pitiable condition and I wish I could help you. But I do not know how. The little knowledge I possess I will tell you." Then he gave him something to eat and spoke to him again, "My son, you must keep straight on and at some distance from here you will come to a body of water over which you must jump. Then you must proceed straight on."

Then the young man arose and continued on his journey. Soon he came to a large body of water that had a very swift current, the water whirling around at a terrific speed. He was afraid to jump across because the land on the other side seemed so small. It looked like the merest speck of green, so small that it had the appearance of a man's eyebrows. Indeed it seemed impossible to jump across but he remembered what the old man had told him and he decided to attempt it. "After all," he thought, "what if anything does happen," and so he closed his eyes and jumped. He landed on the other side and then looked back to see the water. But he could not find it. It was only after looking very carefully that he noticed a very small creek. What he had seen before as a large body of water whirling along at a terrific speed, appeared now as a very small creek. Then he thought to himself: "Perhaps everything that looks difficult to me will in reality be easy," and from this he took courage. Now he felt that he would be able to accomplish what he was seeking.

As he walked along he came to a lodge and in it he found the old man of the previous day with another person just like him. They gave him something to eat and said to him, "Grandson, we will concentrate our attention on the object you have in mind. It is very difficult but since your resolve is so strong you will undoubtedly accomplish it. So go right on and in the next place you will find a friend of ours who will help you. We too shall assist you." Thus they spoke to him.

Then the young man started out again and after a time came to another lodge where he found three old men, two of whom he had seen before, and another. The third one gave him something to eat and spoke to him saying, "Grandson, we are going to help you. You are doing very well. Now do all that we have told you for otherwise you will fail in your quest."

Then the young man started out again and after a while came to a knoll where he found a large gathering. Indeed the place was evidently a large village and there seemed to be no end to it. But strangely enough no people were to be seen; not a person was there anywhere. There were many bark lodges and he peeped into them but they were all empty. Finally he entered one and there he found four old men, three of whom he had met before and a fourth one. The fourth one spoke to him, "Grandson, you have come to the place you have been seeking. Your wife, however, you will not be able to see. Now do what I tell you if you ever wish to see her. To-night there is going to be a big dance which you will attend. Now remember, never turn around. We will take care of you."

In the evening he heard a drum beaten followed by some noise, then a shout here and there. Again he heard the drum beaten and ever greater was the noise. The four men arose and said, "Come, it is about time to start, for otherwise the lodge will be too crowded when we arrive."

They proceeded to the center of the village where they found a long lodge which they entered. The young man they placed in the middle. As he sat there he heard some whispering, "Wakisha has come; he has followed his wife as far as this; he is here. Yet his is a fruitless task, for never will he attain his quest." Then the voice began to annoy him and tease him. "Why his wife is married. Indeed I am the one she has married."

Soon after, the singing started. It was wonderful. All his relatives came and sang their songs. They were singing about him. They were saying, "Wakisga has come for his wife; Wakisga has come for his wife!" Thus they teased him. All night they did this but when the sun rose they all disappeared. His wife did not know anything about it. He returned with the four men to their lodge and there he was congratulated profusely. "You have done well grandson, you have done well, but to-morrow the test will be more difficult. Try your best."

The next evening he heard the drum beat again and after the fourth time, he entered the lodge with the four men. That whole night he was teased and annoyed. The ghosts did everything in their power to make him talk. All sang and the young man thought it was wonderful, more wonderful and exciting than on the previous night. Finally the ghosts began putting their hands on his head, pulling him down and doing all sorts of things to him. He endured it as best he could and finally the day dawned and they all disappeared. He returned with the four men and they cautioned him against the next night.

The third evening had now come. The drum was beaten and the ghosts responded by cheering. At first it was not loud but then it became louder and louder. They entered the lodge. Immediately the ghosts began to tease him and even the six attendants that had been placed at his disposal to help him by the four old men, could do nothing. The singing began again. The young man sat there covered with the blanket and it was hard for him to resist the temptation of turning around. The force of the drumming was simply terrific; it shook the earth with its vibrations. The ghosts tugged at the blanket of the young man, tried to pull him down and fell all about him. At last morning dawned and as the sun rose, they all disappeared. He went home and the old men said to him, "You have done very well. To-morrow will be the last night. It is going to be very hard. There will be eight of us to help you. But even then we will be of no avail unless you too do your best."

Toward evening the drum was beaten again and soon the young man walked to the dancing lodge accompanied by the old men. The village had grow rapidly overnight. There were far more ghosts there than on the previous night for they increased just as the number of deaths on earth increased. The dancing-lodge was already crowded when they got there and they were literally almost trodden upon by the ghosts as they entered. As soon as the young man entered, he heard the voice of his wife saying to him, "Well, if you are going to be indifferent to me there was no need of your coming." He almost turned in her direction as he heard this. Then they began to sing. It was glorious. The earth shook from the vibration of their singing. He was pulled down. His wife was most active in this and always he heard her voice. Wrapped in his blanket he sat there. It was jerked off of him again and again, in spite of all that the eight attendants could do. Finally toward morning he grew tired and weakened. The ghosts grabbed him by the ankles and pulled him along the floor. It seemed almost impossible to endure. At last the sun came up and every one disappeared.

"Come let us go now." It was the voice of one of the old men. "Grandson, you have conquered. From now on, however, this shall never happen again, for Earthmaker has not ordained it so. It is only because I and my friends blessed you that you have been successful. Go now and bring his wife," they said to one of the attendants. She was brought to the young man and the old people spoke to them, "I have blessed you both. Go to your homes now." Then he gave them a drum painted with blue clay. "If any one dies, this drum will bring his soul to you and if a

[54]

soul is about to leave the earth, during illness, this drum will bring it back to you. If you pour tobacco for me and my friends, we will always remember you. Now go home. The ghosts will chase you, for they are wicked. Eight attendants will take you home." Then he gave them some ashes and told them to throw them behind them if necessary.

On their way home they were chased by the ghosts. "Alas, Alas! He has taken our wife away. Let us rescue her!" they shouted. Close they came to the two people but then the young man took the ashes and threw them behind him and the ghosts called to one another saying, "Run away, the ashes will ruin our clothes." They retreated. Again and again this happened but finally the two young people were able to reach the earth.

Coyote Goes on the Warpath

"Come, let us go on the warpath and take Coyote along. He is always up to something foolish, always exaggerating everything he does. Let some one go for him." Then someone went to get him saying, "Coyote, we are going on the warpath. Why don't you come along too?" "Good. Of course I'll go along," and he accompanied the man back to the others. Then each one in turn sang his death song and when it was Coyote's turn he too sang:—

> "Wiyayoho! Wiyayoho!
> The little coyote, if he dies, if he dies,
> Who will weep for him?
> Wiyayoho! Wiyayoho!
> The little coyote, if he dies, if he dies,
> Who will weep for him?"

§7. *The Teachings of My Father*

My father used to keep up the old habit of teaching us the customs of the Winnebago. He would wake us up early in the morning and, seated around the fireplace, speak to us. The girls would be taught separately. Now this is what my father told me:

I

My son, when you grow up, see to it that you are of some benefit to your fellowmen. There is only one way in which you can aid them and that is by fasting. Our grandfather, the Fire, he who stands at all times in the center of our dwelling, sends forth all kinds of blessings. Be sure that you make an attempt to obtain his.

My son, do you remember to have our grandfathers, the war chiefs,[14] bless you. See to it that they have compassion upon you. Then some day as you travel along the road of life, you will know what to do and encounter no obstacles. Without any effort will you then be able to gain the prize you desire. The honor will be yours to glory in, yours without exertion. All the disposable war-blessings belong to our grandfathers, the war-controllers, and if reverently you fast and thirst yourself to death, then these will be bestowed upon you. Yet if you do not wear out your feet in frequent journeyings to and fro, if you do not blacken your face with charcoal, it will be all for naught that you

[14] Symbolical name for all those spirits who were supposed to be in control of war powers.

The Teachings of My Father

inflict this suffering upon yourself. Not without constant effort are these blessings procurable. Try to have one of the spirits created by Earthmaker take pity on you. Whatever he says will come about. If you do not possess one of the spirits from whom to obtain strength and power, you will be of no consequence socially and those around you will show you little respect. Indeed they will jeer at you.

My son, it is not good to die in the village; in your homes. Above all, do not let women journey to the spirit land ahead of you. It is not done. To prevent this from happening do we speak to our sons and encourage them to fast. Some day in life you will find yourself traveling along a road filled with obstacles and then you will wish you had fasted. When such an event confronts you, that you may not find it necessary to reproach yourself, I counsel you to fast. If you have not obtained any knowledge from the spirits, why it may happen that some day, in later life, warriors will be returning from the warpath and as they distribute the war prizes to their sisters,[15] your own sisters will stand there empty-handed envying the rest. But if you obtain blessings from the war-controllers, your sisters will be happy. How proud they will be to receive the prizes, to wear them, and to dance the victory dance! Your sisters too will be strengthened thereby and you will be content and happy.

Now all this it would be well for you to obtain. Try to

[15] Among the Winnebago a man's sisters, especially his elder sisters, were very highly respected and all war prizes, such as wampum-belts, wampum necklaces, etc., were always given to them whenever a man returned from a successful war-party in which he had secured some honor. These war honors were of various kinds. The greatest was considered to be the feat of having struck the body of a dead enemy first.

be a leader of men. To become one, however, is very difficult, the old people used to say. It may happen that you merely pretend to be a leader of men, that you are but a mere warrior in the ranks and yet take it upon yourself to lead a war-party and thus cause a needless waste of life, that you do what is called "throwing away a life." That is the most shameful of all acts. The relatives of the person whom you have thus sacrificed would then have the right to make you suffer, to torture you with burning embers. And then your relatives would have to stand by, sad and humiliated. Not with the blessing of one, not with the blessings of twenty spirits, can you go on the warpath. For that the blessings of all the spirits are necessary—those on this earth, those under it and those who lie pinned through it, the Island Weights; those in the waters and those on the side of the earth, the winds, all four of them. You need the blessings of the spirit who dispenses life from one side of his body and death from the other, the blessings of the Sun, the Moon, the Daylight, and the Earth. All these Earthmaker has made controllers of war and by all these must you be blessed in order to lead a war-party.

My son, if you cast off your dress for many people, that is, if you give to the needy, your people will be benefited by your deeds. It is good thus to be honored by many people. And even more will they honor you if you return victorious from the warpath with one of the four limbs, that is, one of the four war honors. But if you obtain two, or three, or perhaps even four limbs, then all the greater will be the honor. Then whenever a war feast is given you will receive part of the deer that is boiled, either part of its body or part of the head.[16] When on some other occasion,

[16] The meat of a deer at such a feast is given only to great warriors. The head is regarded as the choicest piece.

such as the Four Nights' Wake, you are called upon to recount your war exploits in behalf of the departed souls, be careful, however, not to claim more than you actually accomplished. If you do, you will cause the soul of the man in whose behalf you are telling it, to stumble [17] in his journey to spirit land. If you tell a falsehood then and exaggerate, you will die before your time, for the spirits, the war-controllers, will hear you. It is indeed a sacred duty to tell the truth on such an occasion. Tell less than you did. The old men say it is wiser.

My son, it is good to die on the warpath. If you die on the warpath, you will not lose consciousness at death. You will be able to do what you please with your soul and it will always remain in a happy condition. If afterwards you wish to become reincarnated as human being, you may do so, or you may take the form of those-who-walk-upon-the-light, the birds, or the form of any animal you please, in short. All these benefits will you obtain if you die on the warpath.

II

My son, if you cannot obtain war-blessings, fast at least for position in life. If you fast then, when you get married you will get along well. You will then not have to worry about your having children and your life will be a happy one. If you fast and have the spirits bless you with all that concerns the happiness of your home, then throughout life

[17] According to Winnebago belief the soul of a deceased individual in his journey to spirit land must cross a very slippery, swinging bridge and it is thought that if, during the wake following the man's burial, any of the invited warriors exaggerate their achievements the unfortunate soul will not be able to cross this bridge and will stumble and fall into the abyss of fire over which it is thrown.

you will never be in need of anything. Fast for the food you are to receive. If you fast frequently enough for these things then some day when your children ask for food they will be able to obtain a piece of deer meat without difficulty; they may indeed be able to obtain a piece of moose meat. It lies within your power to prevent your children from ever going hungry.

Now again, my son, let me enjoin you. Do not abuse your wife. Women are sacred. If you make your wife suffer, then you will die in a short time. Our grandmother Earth is a woman, and in abusing your wife you are abusing her. Most certainly will you be abusing your grandmother if you act thus. Since after all it is she who is taking care of us, by your action you will be practically killing yourself.

When you have your home, see to it that whoever enters your lodge obtain something to eat, no matter how little you yourself may have. Such food will be a source of death to you if withheld. If you are stingy about giving food, some one might kill you in consequence; some one may poison you. If you ever hear of a stranger passing through your country and you want to see him, prepare food for him and have him brought to you. In this manner you will be doing good and it is always good to do good, it is said.

If you see a helpless old person, help him if you have anything at all. If you happen to possess a home take him there, and feed him, for he may suddenly make uncomplimentary remarks about you.[18] You will be strengthened thereby. Or perhaps when he comes, he may bring with him under his arms a medicine bundle, something he cher-

---

[18] It is considered exceedingly bad form for a guest to admire anything in the house he is visiting.

ishes very much and which he will offer you. If it is a bulb-medicine keep it to protect your house. Your home will never then be molested by anything evil and nothing evil will enter your house, neither bad spirits, ghosts, disease, nor unhappiness. Now such will be your life if you do as I tell you. Witches will keep away from you. Thus by fasting will you benefit yourself and your fellowmen.

You know that Earthmaker created all the spirits, those that live above the earth, those who live on the earth, those who live under the earth, those who live in the water—all these he created and placed in control of powers. Even the minor spirits Earthmaker placed in control of something. In this fashion he created them and after that, he created us and because we were created last and no further powers were left, he could not put us in control of anything. Then, however, did Earthmaker create a weed and this he placed us in control of. He further told us that none of the spirits he had created would have the power to take this weed away from us without giving us something in exchange. He told us that if we offered him a pipeful of this weed, which we call tobacco, he too would grant us whatever we asked for. Now it so happened that all the spirits came to long for this weed as intensely as they longed for anything in creation and for that reason if, at any time, with tobacco in our hands we make our prayer to the spirits, they will take pity upon us and bestow upon us the blessings which Earthmaker gave them. Indeed so it is, for Earthmaker created it thus.

Fast, my son. If you are blessed by the spirits and then blow your breath upon people who are ill, they will become well. Thus will you help your fellowmen. If you can cure any of your fellowmen of disease, then you will be of even more than ordinary help to them. If you can draw dis-

[61]

ease from out the body, people will greatly respect you. If then you happen to be without work, all that you need for your support they will give you. For as long a time as you live they will do this for you. After your death people will speak about your deeds for all time. During your lifetime they will say, "Yes, he really has power."

If you are not able to fast, do at least try to obtain some power from those individuals who know the virtues and powers of certain plants. It is sad enough, of course, if you will have to admit to yourself that you could not obtain blessings during fasting; but if you could not, at least try to have those who possess the plants I have mentioned, take pity on you. If they take pity on you, they will present you with one of the good plants that give life to man. Now it will not suffice for you to possess merely one plant. You should try to obtain all those plants that grow among the hairy covering of our grandmother, the Earth—all those that give us life—until you have a complete medicine bundle. Then will you truly have reason to feel encouraged.

Some of the medicine men, the shamans, were blessed by the waterspirits.[19] If you wish to obtain really powerful blessings and gain the power of curing many people, you will have to fast a long time and sincerely. If four, or say ten, of the truly powerful spirits bless you, then some day when you have children and anything happens to one of them, you will not have to look around for a medicine man, but all you will have to do will be to look into your own medicine bundle. Search there and you will undoubt-

[19] Waterspirits are mythical animals generally described as having the shape of a lynx or wild-cat and provided with long tails that completely encircle their bodies. Their gifts to man are ambivalent and it depends upon the man whether he cares to make good or bad medicines from their bodies. Their so-called "bones" generally consist of semi- or completely fossilized objects.

edly be able to find the medicines necessary for curing your children. Indeed after a while you will be called upon to cure your fellow men. Then you can open your medicine bundle without embarrassment, for you will have the knowledge necessary for treating the sick. You will know where the disease is lodged and your treatment will be successful, for it was only after the greatest efforts on your part that you succeeded in obtaining the requisite blessings. If you declare to the patient that he will live, then he will live. If you make proper offerings to the medicine and speak to your medicine in the proper manner, it will exert all the power it possesses to cure the patient. Now you must make good offerings to these medicines; you must give many feasts in their honor and then if, in addition, you address them as if they were human beings, they assuredly will help you and do what you ask. You may accordingly accept the payments offered to you by your patients in good conscience and your children will wear these payments in the form of wampum necklaces and thus gain renewed strength. They will be well and happy. These are the reasons why I want you to be extremely careful in your attitude. Medicines are good for all purposes; that is why they were given to us. Earthmaker gave them to us so that we could cure ourselves from disease.

If any one tries to obtain these staffs of life, these medicines and inflicts sufferings upon himself in acquiring them, then assuredly will our grandmother Earth have cognizance of it. She knows all that you have lost in obtaining them and in the long run what you have lost, will be returned to you. You made your offerings for the future and it is good for people to look forward to their future.

Say, you wish to obtain the paint medicine. For that you

would have to put yourself in the most abject condition before the spirits. If you smear yourself with your paint medicine it will irresistibly attract the enemy; it will paralyze him, deprive him of all power of movement and utterly overpower him. Keep it in your home and then you will never be in want of riches. People will give you their most valued possessions owing to the influence of this paint medicine. The paint medicine is made from the blood of the waterspirits and that is why it is so holy. People obtain it by fasting and thirsting themselves to death and then receiving a blessing from the waterspirit. Earthmaker placed the waterspirits in possession of these powers so that they could then, in turn, bestow them on us.

Some people succeeded in obtaining a medicine that will enable a person to outdistance another in running. It might perhaps be well for you to learn something about this. There are medicines to be used in courting; medicines to prevent married people from separating; medicines for getting rich; medicines for causing people to become crazy. Should you, for instance, wish to make a person feel very sad at heart, then you can poison him with this last-named medicine and even make him crazy. It is also possible to make a woman who has refused you become a harlot, for this medicine will make her fall in love with every man she sees. Indeed any kind of medicine you desire can you obtain from certain individuals. Some are acquainted with medicines that put one to sleep, others with those that keep one awake and give one insomnia. Some have medicines enabling one to overcome the viciousness of dogs who are put to watch over women; others again have medicines that make people single out the possessor in a crowd. Every one will look at him and consider him a great man.

The Teachings of My Father

There are medicines to prevent people from getting tired when walking and medicines to cause a dog fight to take place. In short there are medicines for everything.

Every one must take care of himself and try to obtain that knowledge which will enable him to live in comfort and happiness. Try therefore to learn about the things you will need. If you know them, then as you travel along in life, you will not have to go to the expense of buying them from others, but you will have your own medicines. If you act in this way and if, in addition, you fast properly, you will never be caught off guard in life. Should you possess a home, it will look beautiful and you will never be in want. That is why I know you will never regret this that I am telling you. So you shall travel on your journey though life, along the virtuous road taken by all your fellowmen, and your actions and behavior will never become the butt of your neighbor's sarcasm.

Help yourself as you travel along the road of life. The earth has many narrow passages scattered over it. If you have something with which to strengthen yourself, then when you get to these narrow turns you will be able to pass through them safely and your fellow men will respect you. See to it that people like you. Be on friendly terms with every one and then every one will like you. You will be happy and prosperous.

Never do any wrong to your children. Whatever your children ask of you, do it for them. If you act thus people will then say that you are good natured.

If any one in the village loses a friend through death, should you at all be wealthy, cover the expenses of the funeral of the deceased, if you can. Help the mourners likewise in defraying the expenses of feeding the departed. If you act thus, you will do well. All the people you have

[65]

helped will then really know what kind of a man you are. For the good you do people will love you.

It is not good to win at gambling. You may possibly become rich thereby but that is no life to lead. If you are blessed with luck in cards, if you are blessed with luck at gambling, you will perhaps win things and have plenty of wealth, but none of your children will live.

Now if you do all that I have told you, you will lead a happy and prosperous life. That is why we Winnebago preach to a child we love so that it should never become acquainted with the things that are not right, and never do anything wrong. Then if, in later life, a person does anything wrong, he will do it with a clear knowledge of the consequences of his actions.

III

My son, when you get married, do not make an idol of the woman you marry; do not worship her. If you worship a woman she will insist upon greater and greater worship as time goes on. This is what the old people used to say. They always preached against those men who hearken too strongly to the words of women; who are the slaves of women. Now it may happen that a man has received many warnings as to his behavior in this regard and that he pays no attention to them. It may go so far that when he is asked to attend a war-bundle feast [20] he will refuse to go; it may be that when he is married he will listen to the voice

[20] The war-bundle feast was the great war ceremony of the Winnebago. It was given by all those individuals who possessed a war-bundle and since theoretically there was only one war-bundle in each clan, the basis of the organization of the ceremony was the clan. The ceremony consisted largely of prayers, songs and speeches in honor of the spirits more definitely associated with war. For each

The Teachings of My Father

of his wife and refuse to go on a warpath. He might as well have been brought up as a girl. Men who are real men perform the deeds of men, but such a man will never perform a real man's deed. If he should actually attend a war-bundle feast he will be given the leanest piece of meat, only given to a man of no account. Why should any one run the risk of being thus jeered at? Now when a really brave man attends a war-bundle feast he is given a deer's head. This other man gets a lean piece! It will dry up in his throat, so humiliated and disgraced will he feel. After a while he will not be allowed to go to any feast; his wife will not let him. He will listen to the voice of his wife. His relatives will scold him, his sisters will think nothing of him. They will tell people never to go to visit him. Finally when he has become a real slave of his wife he will even hit his relatives if she asks him to. It is for these reasons that I warn you not to listen to women. You will be considered different from others. It is not good.

Remember this too, that women cannot be watched. If you try to watch them and are jealous about them, then your female relatives will also be jealous of them. Finally when your jealousy has developed to the highest pitch, your wife will leave you and run away with some one else. You have allowed her to see by your actions that you worship a woman, and one alone, and, in addition, you have been watching her all the time. Because of this incessant annoyance she will run away from you. If you think that

of these spirits, a buckskin decorated with the symbol sacred to the spirit, was prepared and then at the most dramatic moment of the ceremony these buckskins were thrown out of the ceremonial lodge and it was believed that the spirits came down in person to fetch them. The war-bundle feast was specifically a man's ceremony.

[67]

your wife is the only one to love, you have humbled yourself and she will be taken from you. You have likewise made the woman suffer; you have made her unhappy. The whole world will hear about it. No other woman will want to marry you and you will have the reputation of being a bad man.

Now you may act in the following way: You see people starting on a warpath and you join them knowing that it is an honor to die on the warpath. But you will join them because you feel unhappy at your wife's flight. Now this is not the proper way to act. You are throwing away your life; you are causing the leader of the war-party to throw away a life. If you want to go on the warpath, do not go because your wife has been taken away from you, go because you feel courageous enough to do so.

It is on the warpath that a man has fun! Do not go, however, unless you have fasted adequately. You must fast for each specific warpath. If you do not and yet join a war-party, then in the midst of the fight, a bullet will come your way and kill you. That will happen because you did not fast. If you have performed any deeds of valor, recount them to your sisters and to your sister's children. Those in charge of war-bundles are good to listen to in such matters. Those to whom such people give advice will eat an excellent dish; they will have the honor of sitting near a great warrior in the middle of the lodge.

These are the things of which the old people spoke and this also is the advice I give you. I myself never asked for these things, but my father did. Your grandfather did. He asked for the informatior relating to the manner in which people are to behave. Never, when you are older, should you allow yourself to get in the predicament of not knowing what is the right thing to do. Ask for this instruction, my son. It is not a matter requiring a few moments; it is something that must be thoroughly learned. You, too, must learn it.

To a girl the following was told:

My daughter, as you travel along the path of life, listen to your parents. Do not let your mother work. Attend to the wants of your father. All the work in the house belongs to you. Do not shirk it. Chop wood, pack it; look after the gardens; gather the vegetables and cook them. When you come back to the village in the spring, plant your fields immediately. Never get lazy, for Earthmaker created you to do these things.

My daughter, when you get your menses, do not ask those in the house to give you any food. Fast and do not eat until you get back to the family lodge. If you act thus, you will be fasting for your seat, for your position in life. You can only keep this seat by fasting. Then when you marry, even if your husband has been a good-for-nothing before, he will become a good hunter. You will have accomplished this for him. You will not fail in anything and you will be happy and contented. If, on the contrary, you do not do as I tell you, then when you marry, you will weaken your husband. After a while he will become sickly and it will be your fault.

It is not good to use medicine. If you marry a man and place medicine upon his head, you will weaken him and he will not amount to anything. It may happen that you do not want your husband to leave you and that after reflecting on the matter, you place some medicine on his head, to prevent him from leaving you. This is not good. You will be ruining a man. It is equivalent to killing him. Do not do it. It is forbidden. If you marry a man and want to live with him permanently, work for him in order to hold him. When you marry a man, listen to what he says. If you do your work properly and the man likes you, he will never leave you. By working for him must you make your husband love you. Now remember it is not good to use medicines on him. At least before you are fairly mature in years do not use any, for you will thereby merely weaken yourself and your life will be of no consequence. Indeed you may cause the medicine to work on yourself and then become demented in consequence.

Marry only one man at a time. Be good and virtuous in your married life. If you do not listen to what I am telling you, you will become bad and men will make fun of you. They will do whatever they wish with you; joke with you familiarly on any subject. If you do not listen to me you will injure yourself. Thus did the old people speak to one another and thus did they hand down these precepts from one generation to another, warning young girls against committing wrong actions. They also said that when a girl is growing up, one should admonish her and that is why I am now speaking to you.

As you grow older, when you get to be a young woman, the men will begin to court you. Never hit a man. It is forbidden. If you dislike a man very much tell him to go away gently. If instead, you hit him, remember that frequently young men possess certain injurious medicines which they may use against you. Even if a particular person does not possess them, he knows where to get them. Then this man whom you have humiliated, will use it and transform you from a chaste and nice woman to a loose one, to a harlot. That is why the old people used to warn the young girls not to maltreat a man. Hope with all your heart that you do not fall into such a predicament. I really mean what I say.

Do not be haughty with your husband. Do whatever he says. Kindness will be returned to you and he will treat you in the same way as you treat him.

If you have a child and it is naughty, do not strike it. In olden times when a child was naughty, the parents did not strike it, but instead made the child fast. Then when he is quite hungry he will reflect upon his disobedience. If you hit the child you will merely be putting more naughtiness in him. It has also been said that mothers should not lecture their children, that they merely make them bad by admonishing them. If your husband scolds them, do not take their part for then they will become bad indeed. If a stranger makes your children cry, do not speak to the stranger in your children's presence and take their part, If you wish to take the children's part, prevent such a thing from happening and keep your children home, and there at home, take good care of them and think of the best means of letting your children get to know you. When you are bringing up children, do not imagine you are taking their part if you just speak about loving them. Let them see it for themselves. Let them see what love is by observing you give things away to the poor. Then they will see your good deeds and then they will know whether you have been speaking the truth or not.

Do not show your love for other children so that other people notice it. Love them but let your love for them be different from your love for your own. The children of other people are different from your own and if they were to be taken to some other place they would become estranged from you; they would no longer belong to you.

You can, however, always depend upon the love of your own children because they are of your own body. Love them therefore.

If you do not have any real interest in your husband's welfare and affairs, then you will be to him like any other woman. People will ridicule you. On the other hand, if you pay more attention to your husband than to your parents, if you listen to him more than to them, that will be equivalent to deserting them. Let your husband keep your parents and take good care of them for they depend upon him. Your parents saw to it that you married him and they expect you to make some return for this as well as for the fact that they raised you.

Do not hurt the feelings of your relatives, the old people used to say. If you hurt their feelings you will make your brothers-in-law feel ashamed of themselves on account of the evil things you say about them.

Never desire to have any other man than your husband when you are married. Have only one husband. Do not give any one the right to call you a prostitute.

The old people said, "Never hit your relatives." You may be on bad terms with one of them, for instance, and he may die. Then people will say that you used to quarrel with the deceased when he was alive. They may even claim that you are overjoyed at his death, that you want to dance with joy. Then indeed will your heart be sore and you will think to yourself how best you can make amends. Even should you have a performance of the Medicine Dance given in his honor, if you wish to bury him with honor, even then people will say, "What does all this mean? She used to be partial and jealous when he was alive. Now that he is dead she loves him! She should not do such things. She is merely wasting her wealth. She need not have spent so much." Thus will people speak of you. Then indeed will your heart ache to its very depths. Perhaps you will even get angry when people say these things to you. It is to prevent this from happening that the old people used to say, "Love one another." If you have always loved a person then when he dies you will have the right to feel sorry. All your relatives will love you; indeed every one will love you. If you behave like a true woman you will be beloved by all and then if you meet with some crisis in life, all will turn their hearts to you in your trouble.

It will be good for you if you conduct yourself in the way I have just told you. That is what I wish you to do. In your own home you have doubtless been instructed in all the domestic work, your part in hunting, and in the work around the camp. If you learn about all these matters then some day when you visit your husband's relatives you will not find yourself in an embarrassing position from which you cannot extricate yourself. When you are visiting your husband's people do not walk around in a haughty manner. Do not act as if you were far above them. Try to get them to like you. If they like you they will put you in charge of their camp.

Never think a home is yours unless you make one yourself. If you are living with people and have put them in charge of your household, do not behave as though the home were still yours.

§8. Courting

It was at about this time that I desired and tried to court women. I did not, however, know the proper thing to say. The young men always went around at night to court. During the day I used to mix with the women but when evening came I did not know what to say. I had, however, a brother who was a very handsome man and he offered to take me along so that I could learn. One night therefore I went along with him. We went to a girl who was having her menses at the time, a young girl. At such times the girls are accustomed to live apart from the rest of the family. We were very cautious about the whole matter because these girls were always carefully watched by their relatives. The relatives knew that it was customary for the young men to attempt to court the girls then. Now one of the precautions frequently taken was to pile sticks and branches about the lodge so that it would be difficult to enter. If then a person tried to enter one of these lodges he was likely to make some noise moving the branches and thus awaken the people living in the larger lodges near by. They would, of course, run to see what was the matter.

It was to such a place that we went. After working at the obstacles placed near the entrance for some time,

[74]

my brother succeeded in entering the lodge. I went as close as possible to listen. My brother spoke in an audible whisper so that I could hear. Sure enough, I heard him. However, after lying there for some time I got tired and fell asleep. I began to snore and my brother had to wake me up. Afterwards the girl found out and sent us both away.

After a time I entered the lodges myself. We always had blankets wrapped around us and we took care to have our heads well covered on these occasions.

Sometimes a girl would be acquainted with quite a large number of men and then these would always gather around her lodge at night and annoy her parents a good deal. We would, in fact, keep them awake all night. Some of these people kept vicious dogs.

There was one old woman who always watched her daughter carefully on such occasions. It was a long oblong lodge in which the daughter was confined, with just enough room for two persons. The mother of the girl finally decided to sleep with her daughter. Nevertheless we annoyed her all the time just for her meanness. Once we went there and kept her awake practically all night. Just before dawn, however, she fell asleep, so we young men—there were several of us— pulled up the whole lodge, poles and everything, and threw them into the thicket. The next morning the two women were found sleeping in the open, it was rumored, and the mother was criticized for being overcareful.

The reason why some of the older people were careful at that time was because it had been reported that some young men had forced themselves into lodges where they had not been willingly received.

On one occasion I went to see a young girl and arrived there before the people had retired so I waited near the lodge until they went to sleep. As I lay there waiting, listening, I fell asleep. When I woke up it was morning and when the people got up they found me sleeping there. I felt very much ashamed of myself and the people laughed at me. I was not long in getting away.

We always did these things secretly for it was considered a disgrace to be caught and discovered.

On another occasion, in another place, I was crawling into a lodge when some one woke up as I was about halfway in. I immediately stopped and remained quiet and waited for the people to fall asleep again. In waiting, however, I myself fell asleep. When the people woke me up in the morning I was lying halfway inside the lodge. After waking me up they asked me whether I wouldn't stay for breakfast but I immediately ran away.

After a while I began to go around with some particular girl and I liked it so much that I would not get to sleep at all at night. I would sleep during the day. While we were acting in this manner our parents saw to it that we had food to eat and clothes to wear. We never helped them, for we were always courting girls. Only in the fall, when we picked berries, did we help along. However, as we were generally out all night, we could not do much work even then.

Courting

I used to go out courting and be in the lodges all night and yet, most of the time, I never succeeded in speaking to any of the girls. I did not mind that so much, however, for I was doing it in order to be among the girls. This is what I enjoyed. Indeed I used to go around telling people that I was really keeping company with such and such a girl. I used to say this to my men associates. In reality I did not get much more than a smile from one or two girls. Yet even this I prized as a great thing.

§9. *My Brother-in-Law's Fasting Experience*

Just about this time we moved to the hunting-grounds and I began to fast again. I began to take sweat baths and caused myself to vomit in order to be purged. My father was a good hunter; he was always able to kill many deer and occasionally a bear.

My brother-in-law thought a good deal of me. He was a holy man and a shaman. One day he said to me, "Brother-in-law, I am going to bless you although you will have to fast for it. I was once blessed by four spirits, brothers, called *Good giant-cannibals*. They said that they had never before blessed any one. They promised me that if I ever got into any difficulties they would help me. They blessed me with long life. Now this blessing I will give you. If, for four nights, you fast without a break, these giants will speak to you." Thus he spoke to me. Then he continued, "These four brothers are called *Good-giant, Good-heart, Good-as-he-walks-about, Good-where-he-lifts-his-foot-from*. They lived toward the east, where you will find a promontory. Nothing across the large body of water is too difficult for them to accomplish."

So when I fasted I always offered tobacco to these spirits first. I would cry to these spirits, but I never fasted over night.

§10. *A War-Bundle Feast*

When the hunting was over my father selected ten deer with which to give a war-bundle feast. Those who had been selected as attendants then transferred these deer to the place where the people always give their feasts.

I was fasting at the time and only broke my fast at evening. Every night I went out to make my appeal to the spirits before I ate. Five days before the feast was to be given I commenced to fast through the night also. On the fifth night, together with my older brother, I went to the feast. During the day I had spent the time in the wilderness uttering my cry to the spirits:

"O spirits, here humble in heart I stand, beseeching you."

I was far more thirsty than hungry. I don't believe that either my tongue or mouth were even moist.

That night we held aloft the deerskins that were to be offered to the spirits and we stood there crying piteously. There we wept humbly and those who were to give the feast wept with us, as they extended their holy compassion to us. Then, at midnight, we stood near the war weapons and again raised our appeal to the spirits.

Our feast was given in a lodge that had eight fireplaces. The host always sits near the last fireplace, at the east end. There we stood crying to the spirits. My older brother fell to the ground from fatigue and exhaustion. We were stark naked except for our breech-clouts. When this prayer was finished we put on our moccasins. Then the host greeted the participants as follows:

"I greet you; I greet you all, war-bundle possessors. My grandparents, especially my grandfather, concentrated their minds upon this ceremony for me. The fireplace, the food, the offerings, with which the spirits blessed my grandfather, that I am going to ask for myself to-day. However weakly I may wobble about in trying to do the proper thing to-day, I know that my elders present here will extend their aid to me. I am now going to offer some tobacco to you all. War-bundles possessors, I greet you all."

Following the speech came the prayers to the various spirits:

Hearken O Earthmaker, our father, I am about to offer tobacco to you. My ancestor concentrated his mind upon you and that with which you blessed him I now ask of you directly. I ask for the small amount of life you granted him, aye for four times the blessings you bestowed upon him. May I never meet with trouble in life.

O Grandfather, chief of the Thunderbirds, you who live in the west, here is a handful of tobacco. Extend to me the deer with which you blessed my ancestor. I pray you to accept this tobacco from me. May I never meet with trouble in life.

[80]

A War-Bundle Feast

O Grandfathers, spirits of the night, walkers in darkness, to you I offer tobacco and ask for the fireplaces which my ancestor received. If you smoke this tobacco see to it that I never become a weakling.

To you who live in the south, you who look like a man, you who are invulnerable, you who deal out life from one side of your body and death from the other, you whom we call Disease-Giver, to you I offer tobacco. In daylight, in broad daylight, did you bless my ancestor. With food you blessed him; you told him that he would never fail in anything, you told him that you would avoid his home; you placed animals in front of him that he should have no trouble in obtaining them. An offering of tobacco I make to you that you may smoke it and that I may not be troubled in life.

Then they offered prayers to the Black Hawk, the Sun, the Moon, the South Wind, the Earth, and the Eagle. Many speeches were given, for every guest who was invited to impersonate a spirit delivered one. The man who was impersonating the Thunderbird spoke as follows:

Host and relatives, all you who are seated here, to all I send forth my greetings. All those present have given me good advice and even the women and children here have pleaded in my behalf with the spirits. What love that was! And of what does life consist of but love! The clan counselor is repeating the songs that were obtained when the sacred bundle was made, so that when the time for the tobacco offering to the spirits came, the specially prepared tobacco would be ready. Now indeed that time has arrived and they are all sitting here prepared to pray to all the various spirits. Long before, when in their visions they were vouchsafed a warpath, the soul of the man they were to kill would be already in their possession when they performed this ceremony. It is to attract his soul that this ceremony is performed. You are going to have a good and prosperous warpath. When you are actually in the midst of the warpath and are about to rush upon the enemy, pour tobacco to the various spirits who are in control of war, say, "Thus, grandfathers, were we accustomed to offer tobacco to you." Although you may not know by any word or direct sign whether the war-controllers have answered you, you will know it as soon as the rush upon the enemy takes place, for although you walk where the bullets rain hardest you will pass out of their range and come through in safety. Then when you return to your people every one will rush out to bestow the war honors upon you. If you give this sacred feast in the proper way, if you burn up much tobacco and food, then the various spirits, especially the Thunderbirds who are the greatest war-controllers, will bless you for the excellent way in which you prayed to him. Whenever they pass your way they will remember you. They will even call you by name and say, "Let us smoke here."

This is the way in which young men are encouraged to act, but only a few succeed. It is good. The host has preached to us and pleaded for all those who are present. He has made offerings of food to our grandfathers who live in the west; pleasing offerings of tobacco and buckskin has he sent to them. I have been permitted to impersonate this great spirit and have thus obtained life for myself and my unimportant clansmen, for all of us who have been living in so lowly a condition. With real life have we felt ourselves connected through your actions. We have felt ourselves connected with life by means of that organ which Earthmaker gave us as a measure of things.[21]   I send forth my greetings to you all.

Then he who was impersonating the Disease-Giver spoke:

War-bundle owners, relatives seated around here, I greet you all.   This is indeed a marvelous performance that we have witnessed and he who was able to do it must surely be a marvelous man.   Very few people listen to the advice of their parents but he must have been one who did and that is why he has done so well.   The members of his clan have been sincerely worshiping the spirits.   He who originally made this war-bundle ritual was like a spirit in power and what he told them to do they are doing in every detail.   It is good work they are doing.   Sufficient food are they offering to those in control of war powers for the spirits easily to take cognizance of it.   They have placed ample tobacco and different kinds of buckskin within reach of the spirits.   To you, O Disease-Giver, a pleasing white buckskin has been strung out in offering and with it a pleasing red feather as a hair ornament.   How indeed would it be possible for the spirits not to recognize these offerings? And if they recognize them then we who are impersonating the spirits, will also receive the benefit of the blessings of war and life, extended to the host.

Long ago our ancestors asked the spirits to bless them so that then they might live happily.   Here we are sitting around the fireplace and the life that the host and his friends have asked for, the spirits are not merely extending to them

[21] A very curious circumlocution for stomach. He means, of course, all the food that has been eaten.

but to all those present. In the olden days the old people used to say to the young boys, "You are not able to fast as yet and to offer up proper food to the spirits so as to clear away the weapons held against you." Now just as these older people would have liked, so you are doing. Even I, who am of no consequence, have nevertheless been permitted to impersonate a great spirit. This you have done for me—allowed me to impersonate that spirit who is the bravest of them all, the one who is in control of power whereby an enemy can be killed outright! One side of this spirit's body controls life and the other death. Now they are about to offer to this spirit, the food of a white animal, of a male animal, the dog, as well as a white buckskin, feathers and tobacco—all of them objects that please him very much. To Disease-Giver they are about to extend these things so that therewith they may ask him for war power and life. It is an awe-inspiring spirit to whom they have been making offerings. Surely I, who have been listening only by virtue of the host's generosity, do not have to say anything in his behalf. He thought of his ancestor when he asked me to impersonate this spirit. Of all the spirits his is the name which one cannot speak lightly, it is said. If nevertheless I greet his name and speak about this spirit, may I not be weakened by uttering it. Those who are about to offer you food, grandfather Disease-Giver, send you their greetings. To you, O host, do I send my greetings, as well as to all the war-bundle owners seated here.

The feasters sang dancing songs throughout all this time. At dawn we were to pass the deerskin offerings through the roof of the lodge. My older brother took the lead. I followed and the others came up behind me. We all had a deerskin apiece. Only those who were giving the feast had the right to hold one of the ten deerskins. A man playing a flute taken from a war-bundle marched ahead, and behind came the people carrying the incense of the burning cedar leaves. We thus marched around the lodge and my brother and I again made our cry to the spirits. At that time we were naked apart from our breech-clouts and moccasins. Four times did we make the circuit. Then we passed the deerskins up through the roof of the lodge.

Now the feasters were to eat again. A separate kettle had been put on for us boys and we were to eat first. They then called upon a man to eat out of our plate with us. His name was *Blue-sitter.* He was a holy man, a shaman, a brave man, one who had obtained many war honors. Four deer ribs were dished out to me in a wooden bowl. Then the one who was to eat out of my plate came and sat near my dish and began to handle the food. He tore it into small pieces and began telling me of the blessing he had received from the spirits. He told me how all the great spirits had blessed him—the Sun, the Moon, the Thunderbirds, the Earth, the Sky, the Daylight, and all the spirits that exist in the heavens. The spirits on the earth and those under the waters, all these talked to him, he said. While partaking of my food he would think of this power, he told me. I would go through battle unharmed and I was to obtain war honors. My children, if I had any, were to enjoy a good and happy life. Thus he spoke.

Then he took a piece of my food in his mouth and placed some in my mouth four times. I continued eating as the rest of the feasters began their meal. For quite some time I was not able to eat much.

Through it all I was not in the least conscious of any dreams or blessings. All that I was aware of was that all the people around me were taking pity upon me. Throughout it all I had my mind fixed on women. In doing these things I imagined that I had accomplished something great and that I had risen greatly in women's estimation. Even though I tried to render myself pitiable in the sight of the spirits, yet through it all, my thoughts were centered upon them. I was never lowly at heart and never really desired the blessing of the spirits. All that I thought of was that I was a great man and that the women would regard me as a great man.

§11. *Wandering and Hunting*

After a while I used to get into the habit of going to town. When I got there I would look into the barrels to see if there was any food in them and if there was I would fill my pockets with whatsoever I found. I used to steal a great deal.

About springtime we always moved away from the vicinity of the town. We always moved to the place where my father intended to trap, generally to the neighborhood of some farming community where there were few Indians. There my mother used to make baskets and sell them to the farmers. We also used to circulate a written petition asking for any help people cared to give us. Whenever they went on this kind of a trip I always went along with them, for sometimes people would take pity on us and give us some old clothes. Sometimes we would even get a good meal at some farmer's house. For these reasons I was always envious of those who went along on such journeys.

Occasionally when we got many provisions I had to carry some of them, but I never minded that. When the birds returned north father used to make us bows and arrows and we would then shoot at them and often kill many. We also used to kill squirrels which my grandmother roasted for us. My older brother was a good shot and I was greatly his inferior. He often killed pheasants.

Whenever the older people went to town circulating petitions for help we youngsters always went along. We always took our bows and arrows with us for the Whites wanted to see how well we could shoot. Often they placed five-cent pieces on some object at a considerable distance and had us shoot at them. We generally hit a number. I would also let my brother shoot at twenty-five cent pieces that I held between my fingers and he never hit my fingers. We would often make as much as five dollars in this way and this money we always gave to our parents.

In summer the Winnebago would return to Black River Falls (Wisconsin). We used to go out with our bows and arrows and stay out all day. At evening when we returned we of course always expected to get a scolding and we therefore had a good excuse ready. It really would have been much better had we returned earlier in the day, but we were enjoying ourselves so much hunting that night overtook us when we were still a long distance from home. Often we would not eat anything at all all day, but to that we were accustomed. Sometimes we would go fishing on a stream nearby, forget all about the time, and then return home very late. We got a scolding then even although we had a good excuse.

§12. *My Grandfather Adopts Me*

Once my father gave me away. Once on my return home I found my father talking to my grandfather and after a while I saw the old man weep. He had just lost a son, a young man and the last of his children. They had all died. It was this that they were talking about. I heard my grandfather say finally that he was tired of life. Then my father, weeping, called him by his relationship term and said: "I sympathize with you for you indeed speak the truth, yet in spite of it all I wish you to live. Here is my son, my own, and of all my children the one I love best. He is obedient. He is present here listening to me. He shall be your companion and as long as you live he will take you by the hand." Thus did he speak and the old man thanked him profusely.

After that I stayed with my grandfather. He thought a great deal of me and I got along very well in every way. He was a great man, one who doctored and who had great knowledge of medicine. This he used to give to the sick. He was also a great Medicine Dance man and an old soldier.

About this time a school was built at Tomah, Wisconsin, and I wanted very badly to go to it. My grandfather consented and I went there for a winter. In the spring of the year my father came after me and asked the superintendent whether I could go home for two weeks and he consented to let me go.

Then my father spoke to me, "My son, your grandfather is dead and they are going to have a memorial ceremony in his honor to take place at a performance of the Medicine Dance. Some one, you know, must take his place in the ceremony and they have decided that I am to be the one. Now, my son, of all the children I possess I have most control over you. I have never kept anything from you and you have never willfully disobeyed me. I want you therefore to do me the favor and take my place. I am getting old and besides cannot control my desire for drink any longer. Under these circumstances I would not be able to live up to the teachings of the lodge. I wish therefore to turn my right over to you. Do you take your grandfather's place." Thus my father spoke to me.

§13. *A Funeral in the Thunderbird Clan*

My grandfather was buried in the manner customary in the Thunderbird clan. His relatives got some one to bury him and the chief mourner invited a distinguished person to talk to the corpse before it was dressed for burial. The person addressed the body as follows:

You are about to leave your relatives. They will remain on earth, objects of pity to all. You must proceed on your road and turn to your left after you start. Continue until you come to the one who is in charge of spirits. When you see him, make the following request—that he bestow upon us all that you fell short of in this world. The means of offering, the tobacco, which Earthmaker gave us, we have given you to take along. As you go along you will come to a place where the road branches off. Do not turn to the right for that leads to the bad spirits. Turn to the left and soon you will come to a guard. Point your pipe at him and he will be thankful. This man will wear a complete suit of clothes and he will be terrible to look upon. He will smoke with you and you must address him as follows: "Grandfather, before I left earth the people told me to ask you to point out which road I was to travel in." Then he will tell you and you will pass ahead and come after a while to a fire on both sides of the earth. The man in charge of it will wear a complete suit of clothes just like the former one. Point the stem of your pipe toward him and he will be very thankful and smoke your pipe. Then make your request—that you be permitted to pass—and he will grant it. As you continue you will come to a round lodge where you will find an old woman. Point your pipe at her and she will permit you to go ahead. Your hair will now have become white but you will not be unconscious. On the contrary you will be in complete possession of your senses. Then you will come to the place where he who is in control of all the souls sits. Go toward him and point your pipe at him. When he is smoking it ask him to show you the road to Earthmaker, our father, and he will point it out to you. Then you must proceed until you come to Earthmaker. When you get to him, point the stem of your pipe toward him and if he takes it and smokes it you must say, "Earthmaker, our father, you know very well what kind of a life I have led." Then he will answer, "My son, you have done well."

After this speech the body was dressed by the person who was to do the actual burying. The best clothes of the deceased were put on, beads placed around his neck, bracelets on his wrist, rings on his fingers and earrings in his ears. It was then placed in the casket.

When the grave-diggers completed their work, the mourners blackened their faces with charcoal and the corpse was taken up by the man to whom this duty was assigned. The mourners followed behind weeping. Thus they proceeded to the grave. When they got there the corpse was immediately placed in it. Then the chief mourner stepped across the center of the grave and the others did the same. When they started back for home they were told under no circumstances to turn around and look in the direction of the grave.

As soon as they returned home the man in charge of the funeral arrangements went around the village and invited every one to come to the wake. Brave men and warriors are especially welcome.

The mourners prepared food and when the sun went down the chief mourner took a stick made of hard wood, lit it, and carried it to the grave, placing it at the east end. It must be still burning when put there. After this the man returned and the funeral manager prepared everything for the feast. When all were gathered around he rose and addressed the people as follows:

Relatives, all you who are gathered around here, I greet you. I have done nothing of any consequence which could justify you in coming here and thus honoring me, but being relatives of mine, you came in the kindness of your hearts to comfort me. I have prepared cooked food and boiled water for the dead person. Tobacco is also handy and as soon as the attendant is ready he will pass this around to those who wish any.

It is good that so many of you have come to-night. You know that we are not creating any new ceremony but are simply following what our ancestors found to be true and good. And as it is said that we should not weep aloud, you will not hear any of us making utterings of sorrow. And even though we weep silently, should any one come to us we will look upon them smiling. We therefore beg of you, should you find us happy in mood, not to think the worst of us.

Then the attendant took the water and tobacco and gave it to the one who was to speak to the soul of the departed person. This one then rose and spoke as follows:

To-night we have come together not for the sake of amusement but because we are afflicted with grief. Now it is the custom to speak to the soul of the departed. It is a sacred action yet even I, they tell me, can do it provided no worthier person can be found. I have even been told that my words will not cause the spirit of the departed to lose his way on his journey to spirit-land. For that reason I am going to speak to the soul of the departed and say the best I can. I greet you all.

Then he takes some tobacco in his hand and passing it behind him through the lodge says:

Here it is, the tobacco. I am certain that you, O ghost, are not very far away, that in fact you are standing right in back of me, waiting for me to reach you the pipe and tobacco, that you might take it along with you; that you are waiting for the food to take with you on your journey. For four nights, however, you will have to wait here. Now here are the things that you desire. In return we ask you to act as mediator between the spirits and us. You have made us long for you and therefore do you see to it that all those things that belonged to you, all those things that you would have enjoyed had you lived longer—the victories on the warpath, earthly possessions, life—that all these you leave behind for your relatives to enjoy. This do you ask for us as you travel along. One thing more do I ask of you: do not cause us to follow you, do not cause your relatives any fear. I have now lit the pipe for you.

[94]

A Funeral in the Thunderbird Clan

Then the pipe is passed on to all those present. After that the leader drinks a little water and passes this around too. It is only after pipe and water have passed all the way around that the people begin to eat. When the meal is over the attendant takes the pipe and some tobacco and places it before some distinguished warrior who has been invited to the wake. The latter is then asked to speak to the soul of the deceased and tell him the route to take on the journey to the spirit land. This warrior then rises and speaks:

Ho, I greet you all. We are not greeting one another because we are happy as on ordinary occasions but because it is the custom to come together at a wake. Now I shall show the soul of the departed the route he is to take and the care he must observe on his journey. I shall announce to him the ghosts over whom I have control and who are to conduct him safely to his destination. I will not exaggerate [22] when I speak of my war exploits but relate only what really happened to me. It is said that if a person exaggerates and tells falsehoods in recounting his exploits on such an occasion, the soul of the departed will stumble on his journey. I shall therefore only tell the truth and I shall tell the chief of the spirits to guide our dead one safely over all obstacles. Now I am not going to speak of anybody else's exploits but only of my own. Only those over whom I have control will I put at the disposal of our dead one to act as his guide. The spirit-tobacco, the spirit-food, and the fire, these things the ghosts over whom

[22] For the dangers of exaggeration on such an occasion see note 15. It was also believed to cause the death of the warrior who indulged in it.

[95]

I have control will carry for him, and they will lead him by the hand until he reaches his destination. I greet you all.

Then he narrated his war exploit. He went into great detail. He told as accurately as it was possible how he had killed a man, broken his collar bone and then flayed him; how he had then chopped and cut up the body and mutilated him in such a fashion that he could not be identified; how finally he had stolen his dogs. All night he spoke in this strain. He went on to tell how he had killed and utterly destroyed an entire village so that no one was left to tell of the massacre. All night he told of his war exploits. Sometimes such an account may last two to three hours. When he finished the people all went to sleep.

For three nights the same thing was repeated. Throughout this time a burning ember was placed at the grave. When the spirit was ready to start his journey he took this ember, it is believed.

For the fourth night all the brave men as well as everybody else in the neighborhood were invited. A great quantity of food was prepared and the relatives of the mourners brought objects to be used in the games that are always played at the wake. They tried to comfort the main mourners as much as possible. On the fourth night a burning ember was also placed at the grave of the deceased.

As soon as the attendants prepared the food the chief mourner got up and spoke:

[96]

A Funeral in the Thunderbird Clan

I greet you all. I know that I am not performing any great action in greeting you. I was in trouble and all my relatives have come to comfort me. You have all asked me to live and not to succumb to my sorrows and I shall therefore try to overcome my grief and sorrow. I will not forget all the good you have done for me. You have been a comfort to me and you have helped me in many things. Now we have come to the last night and I am glad that it is a nice night for the warriors to relate their experiences. If they should say something funny I hope that you will not hold back laughter. I, too, will laugh with you. You are free to make all the noise you care to for I shall feel all the better if you do. This is what I want you to remember. I greet all those who are present here.

Then the one who is to address the spirits speaks:

I greet you all. We have come to this wake for a purpose, much as I would wish that the occasion for it had never happened. Now I am going to tell the soul of the departed the road he is to take, nor will I, by my words, cause him to go astray. On an occasion like this not every one is qualified to speak to the souls of the dead; not every one can do it. My grandfather obtained the right to do it and handed it down to my father, who in turn, turned it over to me. Now I am going to breathe upon the soul of the departed and I wish all those present to do the same. It is said that for those who do not make this breathing it is a sign that they will die. So do all of you breathe with me.

Then he said *ha-a* and all joined with him in repeating it. He now began his address to the spirit of the deceased:

Crashing Thunder

Ho-o! Are you ready? I am going to speak of the Four Nights' Wake during which you listened to your relatives and to the words they had to say. I am placing the sacrificial tobacco in the rear of the lodge.

I suppose you are not far away, that indeed you are right behind me. Here is the tobacco and here is the pipe which you must keep in front of you as you go along. Here also is the fire and the food which your relatives have prepared for your journey. In the morning when the sun rises, you are to start. You will not have gone very far before you come to a wide road. This is the road you must take. As you walk along you will notice something on your road. Take your war club and strike it and throw it behind you. Then go on without looking back. As you proceed you will again come across some obstacle. Strike it and throw it behind you and do not look back. Still farther, you will come across some animals and these also you must strike and throw behind you. Go on right along and do not turn back. The objects you have thrown behind you will go to the relatives whom you left behind on earth. They will symbolize victory in war, riches, and food-animals. When you have gone but a short distance from the last place where you threw an object behind you, you will come to a lodge. This lodge you may enter. One of its doors faces the rising sun. As you enter you will find an old woman on your right. Go and sit opposite her. Then your great-grandmother will say to you, "My great-grandchild, what did the people say to you when you were leaving, when your life was over." And you must answer, "My great-grandmother, as I listened to my beloved relatives they said very little indeed. They said that I was breaking their hearts in leaving them and that they hoped that none

[98]

would follow me soon. Then they asked me to make the following four requests:

First: I was to ask for life; that the flames from the lodge fire rise straight upward. Yet they would be satisfied, they said, if at my departure the flames only swayed to and fro.

Second: Whatever fruit had been predestined for me and that I did not taste, my relatives were not to be deprived of.

Third: They also mentioned nuts, all kinds of herbs, all serviceable hides and skins, all medicinal roots and grasses. They asked me to make a request for all the things that grow on the earth.

Fourth: That if any one had a friend his weapon might have a keen edge on one side.

Now, my great-grandmother, these are the requests my relatives commanded me to make."

Then she will answer you and say, "My great-grandchild, you are wise beyond your years. My great-grandchild, my lodge is a place where all who enter must pass an examination. Earthmaker looks upon it as a keen-edged instrument. No clouds of ill omen ever pass over it. The four requests you have made will be granted. The nuts and herbs you have asked for shall be given to you. There will be nothing of that food predestined for you that your relatives will not taste. The hides and skins, all the grasses, they shall possess in plenty. And if they have friends their weapons will be keen on one side. All that they have requested through you will be granted. Now, great-grandson, here is some food for you in this wooden bowl."

If you eat it you will have a headache. She will say,

"Great-grandson, you have a headache. Let me cup it for you." Then she will break open your skull and take out your brains and you will forget all about your people. You will become like a holy spirit. Your thoughts will not extend as far as the earth, as there will be nothing carnal about you.

Now be sure that you only take a taste and push the dish away from you for then the old woman will say, "My great-grandchild, all that you have left behind you in that dish represents the vegetable kingdom on the earth. Many who are older than you ate all that I gave them. You have a wise head on young shoulders. All that you have left on the plate will grow on the face of the earth. Now Earthmaker is waiting for you in great expectation. There is the door to the setting sun." On your way you will come to the lodge of the chief of the bad spirits and his fire. Those who come, the souls of the brave men who have come from the land of the spirits, will meet you here and touch you. There the road will branch off toward your right and you will see the footprints representing the footprints of those who have passed into life again. Step into their steps and plant your feet upon their footprints, but be careful that you do not miss any. Before you have gone very far you will come into a forest of bushes alternating with prairies. Here in this beautiful country the souls whose duty it is to gather together the other souls, will come to meet you. Walking on each side of you they will conduct you safely home, to Earthmaker. Here the inquiry that took place in the first lodge will be repeated* and answered in the same manner. Then Earthmaker will say to you, "All that your great-grandmother has told you is true. Your relatives are waiting for you in great expectation. Your home is waiting for you."

A Funeral in the Thunderbird Clan

The door of your home will be facing the midday sun. Here you will find your relatives gathered. Then, inasmuch as our ruler will nod assent and express his approval by word of mouth, so shall we do the same.

Then all those assembled at the wake shout *Ho-ha*.

§14. *Initiation into the Medicine Dance*

The person who had died and whose place I was to take was an uncle of my father's. I was glad of the opportunity for I had always liked the Medicine Dance whenever I had seen it. I had aways enjoyed watching from the outside what was taking place inside and I had always been filled with envy. So naturally I was very glad to join and anxious as to what would happen. We proceeded to the place where the ceremony was to be held, traveling from Tomah to Wittenberg. Sometimes we would have to walk, but I enjoyed it nevertheless. I was very happy.

Finally we arrived at the place and my father explained to the people that he had turned over his right of membership to me. They were quite satisfied.

We were to build the ceremonial lodge immediately, so we went and cut the poles for it after measuring the length required. Of course, we hunted around and got the kind of poles always used for that purpose. Then we constructed the lodge. We stuck the poles in the earth. We worked together with three old men, brothers of the man who had died. They told me that this ceremony was a holy affair, that it was Earthmaker's play. We made an offering of tobacco at every move we made. I, of course, thought that it must indeed be a marvelous thing and I was very happy about it. What I was most eager to see was myself killed and then brought to life again in the lodge, as it was believed happened to the members of the Medicine Dance. I also realized that a member of the Medicine Dance, whether man or woman, was different from a person not belonging to it and I was quite anxious not to be an ordinary person any longer but to be a medicine man.

As soon as we finished building the ceremonial lodge the ceremony began, and the first thing the people did was to sing. Then the leader of the band that was giving the dance arose and delivered a speech:

All those who are sitting here I greet. We are waiting for all of you to have compassion upon us. Nephew,[23] I shall now tell you the road you are to travel. He whom we call nephew, the hare, the founder of the Medicine Dance, obtained this life-ensuring ceremony for us. This is the only life; no other exists. Exert yourself to follow in the road of your ancestors and adhere to the ceremony that represented their mode of life. I know you will hearken to what I say. Assuredly you will listen, for thereby you will help and benefit yourself and, at the same time, attain the good life.

Never do anything wrong. Do not steal. Do not quarrel. If on any occasion you meet a woman on the road, turn to the right, never to the left. No matter who the woman is, do not take liberties with her. This is what the old people taught us and if you perform the rites of this ceremony you will obtain the life that we desire for you.

[23] The person to be initiated is always called nephew.

I beg of you to try with all your powers for I wish you to lead a happy life. This truly is our sincere wish.

Ancestors, we greet you. Our ancestors long since departed, performed the ceremony just as we do to-day. We are to have a tear-pouring ceremony for the spirit of the one who has died. All those who are here will mourn for him. Whatever it is that his ghost can obtain for us by his requests,—all that he left behind him in this world—beseechingly we shall ask him to obtain. It is said that this is always procurable. What we mean is additional life. All that our ancestors desired, that we too earnestly desire. So it is when the ceremony was first established. Now we shall sing a mourning song. We must sing it with sincerity and when we cry we must not allow our voices to quaver. It has been said that if a man is bad his crying will be insincere. Ancestors, we greet you.

The first night they kept me up all night and I heard a good deal about sacred affairs. I was not sleepy at any time during the night and I remained this way until morning. I enjoyed it all so much that I did not even go to sleep the next day. The next night they kept me up again but as before I did not get sleepy. On this night they told me even more things. Throughout three successive nights I did not sleep at all. On the fourth night they sang till morning. On the fifth night they were to have what is called the rehearsal. During the day many people began to gather. In the afternoon only the old men and myself went to the sweat lodge. Only the men who had received special invitations were allowed. When we came out it was sundown. Then those occupying the eastern

The Medicine Dance

seat in the main lodge stopped singing and the specially invited people entered the regular ceremonial lodge.

The older people took charge of me for the whole night. Whenever they referred to me they would say, "In the morning when he-for-whom-we-desire-life becomes like us." They meant me and they meant that I would be a member in the morning. So I was extremely anxious for the morning to dawn. All night they danced. This part of the ceremony is called the rehearsal or trial performance.

The next morning, just before day, even while the dance was still going on, the leader of the first and second band, those of the east end and some others, took me to a secret place in the brush. When we got there we found a place where the ground had been cleared in the outline of the dance lodge. There the older people preached to me and told me that the most fearful things imaginable would happen if I made public any of the affair, *i.e.*, told the secrets of the Medicine Dance. The world would come to an end, they said. They told me that if I didn't keep everything secret I would die.

It was in the brush that the leader told me of the road that all medicine men travel.

The Road of Life

My son, as you travel along this road do not doubt it. If you do you'll be unhappy; you'll injure yourself. But if you do everything that I tell you well it will benefit you greatly.

[105]

My son, the first thing you will come to as you travel along, will be a ravine extending to the very ends of the world on both sides. It will look as though it could not possibly be crossed. When you get there you will think to yourself, "Grandfather said that I was nevertheless to pass across." Plunge right through and you will get to the other side.

Now this ravine means that sometimes in life you will lose a child and thoughts of death will come to you. But if you pay attention to my teachings you will be able to go right on and find the road of the lodge on the other side. If you don't try to go beyond, if you get frightened and dwell upon your hardship too much, this will be your grave.

After you have crossed the ravine you will see the footsteps of the medicine men who have gone before you, marked very plainly in the road. Step into them and you will feel good. Then as you go along you will come to an impenetrable brushwood of stickers, thorns, and weeds. You will not see how you can possibly get around them. Then you will remember that your grandfather said that you would be able to penetrate them. This too, you will pass.

The impenetrable brushwood means death. Some one you have loved greatly, but not your wife, will die. You must try to get through this obstacle, not get frightened and not dwell upon your hardship too much. Otherwise this will be your grave.

As you pass along this road, evil little birds will continually din into your ears and will cast their excrement upon you. It will stick to your body. Now don't try to brush it off and don't pay any attention to it. If you pay attention to it you might forget yourself and brush it off and that is not right, and life is not obtainable in this manner.

[106]

The Medicine Dance

The evil birds signify the following. The fact that you have joined the medicine lodge means that your intentions are to lead a good life. Now as soon as you join, the work of evil tattlers will begin and they will say that you have done things contrary to the teachings of the lodge. Perhaps a piece of bird's excrement will fall on you. What of it? Don't brush it off without thought. Some will claim that you had said that the lodge was no good. Yet even then you must not blurt out, "Who said that?" and get angry. Keep quiet and hold your peace.

As you go along you will come to a great fire encircling the earth and practically impossible to cross. It will be so near that it will scorch you. Remember then that your grandfather had said that you would be able to pass it. Plunge through it. Soon you will find yourself on the other side and nothing will have happened to you.

Now this great fire means death. Your wife will die. Go through this as well as you can; don't get discouraged. This fire will be the worst thing you have to go through. You will have been living happily and then without warning your wife will die. There you will be with your children. Remember, however, what your grandfather said and plunge straight through. On the other side you will find the footprints of the medicine men.

After a while you will come to tremendous perpendicular bluffs which hardly seem passable. Think, however, of what your grandfather said and soon you will find yourself on the other side quite safe.

Now these bluffs mean death. As you travel along the road of life you will find yourself alone. All your relatives, all your loved ones, are dead. You yourself will begin to think to yourself, "Why, after all, am I living?" You will want to die. Now this, my grandson, is the place where most encouragement is given for it is most necessary. This is the most difficult of all the places you will come to. Keep in the footprints of the Medicine Dance man and you will be safe. The teachings of the lodge are the only road; they alone will enable you to pass this point safely.

Soon you will come to a hill and when you reach the foot of the hill you will sit down to rest and eat. You will eat dried ribs of bear meat mixed with spirit-food and this spirit-food will vibrate with life. When you are finished you must climb to the top of the hill and look behind you. There will be no one. But in front of you, you will see many people.

Now this hill means that you have reached that period of life where, because you have always done things correctly, you will be continually partaking of feasts. You will always be invited. The road full of people in front of you represents the members of the lodge who have passed before you. There is no one behind you because you are just beginning to enter on that road.

Soon you will come to another hill. It will look like a nice country full of red stone. There you will find food and you will eat out of a very greasy kettle. When you're finished, climb to the top of the hill and you'll see that some people are now following you and that the number in front will be smaller.

You'll be traveling through better country now, i.e., you'll be taken better care of.

Then as you go along, another hill will loom in sight. You must go toward it and there you will find yourself in a country of red willows and bulrushes. Many presents will you find scattered all along this most pleasing of lands. There you will find your food and when you have partaken of it, ascend as far as the middle of the hill. There as you rest you will see a reddish haze across the land. Then go to the top of the hill. As you look behind you will see many people following you and only a few in front.

Halfway up the hill, we have said, the land will be covered with a red haze. This is the Indian summer and this means that you will now have reached that period in life where your eyes have become dim. The red willows, etc., signify that your hair has become grizzled. The men in front of you are the older members of the lodge who will assist you by inviting you to the lodge and those in back of you are the younger members who will give you feasts in order to obtain increased knowledge.

Then finally you will come to a fourth hill. This will be a very beautiful country with white poplars everywhere. There, after having eaten at the foot of this hill, you'll climb it and look around. You will see not one ahead of you and very many people following. The place from which you had started, apparently a long time ago, will seem very near. You will have to rest four times before you get to the top of this hill.

This means that when you get to the fourth hill, you will be so feeble that you will have to rest four times before you succeed in getting to the top. The fact that you see no one in front of you on the road means that you have now become the oldest member of the lodge.

As you walk along you'll come to an oval lodge. There you will find a man who will ask you, "Grandson, how have you acted in life?" You must answer, "I don't know." He will answer and say, "Grandson, I know. Take some food." You'll find four dishes and you must take a spoonful of each. When you have swallowed the fourth spoonful your body will be like that of a dog or a flea, i.e., you will be so old that your body will not only be flat but your ribs will be caved in. The man talking to you will be the one in charge of the medicine-lodge road. You will now become unconscious but not for a long time, i.e., although you will die, you'll go right on in the spirit. Near you, you will find the medicine man's staffs or ladders. The ladders reach to heaven. On the right side you will find a tree, all twisted and slippery from incessant rubbing. On the left you will see a red cedar tree, all smoothed down from wear and dirty from incessant handling. You must grab these trees, and then when you have ascended them you'll come to a country situated right below the place where Earthmaker lives. This country has been especially provided for those who have adhered to the ritual of the Medicine Dance. You will be told that this is your home and, after a while you'll be directed to a long lodge where you will find all those of your relatives who have adhered to the teachings of the lodge. Although you are a grown-up person you will nevertheless be taken on each one's lap in turn. This country is a very happy one to live in. No one is ever in want; no bad clouds float over it; there is no night and there is no work.

After a while the attendants of Earthmaker will come to you and take you to him. There you'll see him face to face. He will tell you that you have done well and that you can become reincarnated in whatever tribe you desire. Those that perform the ritual properly believe that they can come to the world again after death.

After the old man had finished telling about the road of the Medicine Dance Lodge I was shown how to fall down and lie quivering on the ground and how to appear dead. I was very much disappointed for I had

had a far more exalted idea of the shooting. "Why, it amounts to nothing," I thought. "I have been deceived. They only do this to make money." I also thought then that many of the sacred things about which they had spoken to me were not true either. However I kept on and did as I was told for I had been taught to deceive in the ceremony in the brush. As soon as I was proficient in the act of feigning death, we started back to the main lodge.

The older people told me that I would become like them in body as soon as I became a member of the lodge, but I did not experience any change within me. All that I felt was that I had become a deceiver in one of Earthmaker's creations.

During the day, at the regular meeting, I did as I had been taught. Many speeches and many songs were sung and then, at about ten o'clock, the leader of the north band arose and told the story of the origin of the world and of the Medicine Dance.

The Story of the Origin of the World

What it was our father sat on when he came to consciousness we do not know. His tears flowed and he began to cry. Not long was he sunk in thought. He saw nothing and nothing was there anywhere. He took something from the thing on which he was lying and out of it made a portion of our earth. This he sent to the space below him and from where he lay he could see that what he had created had become similar in shape to our earth. Yet nothing grew upon it and it was entirely without a covering. It was not quiet and kept spinning around continually.

Suddenly he thought, "Now if I do the following it will stop." So he made a covering of hair for it. He took something that was like a weed and made grass, and this he sent earthward. Then again he looked at what he had created. It was not quiet but kept spinning around and around. Then he thought to himself, "Well, I must try another way." He took a tree and sent it earthward and again looked at his creation but it was still spinning around and around. Then he made four men and these he sent to the earth, placing one in the east, one in the north, one in the west, and one in the south. Again he looked at his creation. It was still spinning around and around. "Perhaps it will become quiet in the following way," he thought. So he made four beings that we call the *Island Weights*. They were waterspirits. Then he scattered a female spirit over the earth. By this we mean stones. Then finally he looked at his creation and he saw that the earth had become quiet.

He had sent the stones clear through the earth, throughout its whole extent. Only the heads, the tops of the stones, were visible above the ground. He looked at his creation and he saw that the earth had indeed become quiet. No clouds appeared anywhere, the light of day appeared motionless, and the vibrations of heat seemed like floating spider webs drifting past.

All the birds that were to roam over the sky, all the four-footed animals that were to live on this earth, all the animals who were to live below the surface of the earth, all these he placed in lodges that he constructed for them. Then he created the various insects that were destined to live on the earth. Finally at the very end of his thinking

The Medicine Dance

he created us human beings. We were not however even equal in strength to a fly. We were the weakest of all. Then Earthmaker looked at what he had created and liked it and sat filled with happy thoughts.

He was proud of us and gazed again and again at what he had created. He had, however, made the human beings not equal in strength to the other beings and they were on the point of being destroyed by the bad spirits. Then he formed a being in our likeness and when he finished him he called him Foolish-one. Him he addressed as follows: "*Foolish-one,* to the earth you are to go. Weak, pitiable in all respects, have I made the human beings. I made them as my last thought. Now this creation of mine, they the evil spirits are likely to injure. So do you, O *Foolish-one,* go and put things in order."

Then he sent him to the earth. But when *Foolish-one* came there he did not do what he had been told. Indeed he went around the earth doing nothing. He was as useless as a child crawling around on all fours. He really amounted to nothing. Though sent by Earthmaker he amounted to nothing. He did no good and injured the creation of Earthmaker, so Earthmaker took him back and placed him to the right of himself.

Then he made another being in human semblance and when he finished him he called him *Turtle.* "The two-legged-walkers whom I created as the last of my thoughts, evil spirits are about to exterminate. Do you, O *Turtle,* go and put the earth in order." Turtle went and took along with him a knife. When he came on earth he led people on the warpath and he did not look after Earthmaker's creation. So Earthmaker took back the second man and placed him at his left.

Then he made a third being in human semblance and

[113]

when he finished him he named him *Bladder*. To him he spoke, *"Bladder,* you are to go to the earth. As my last thought I created the two-legged-walkers and they were pitiful to behold in every way. They are now on the point of being exterminated and you must save them. Try with all your strength.

When *Bladder* came to the earth he made a long lodge and he created twenty men. That many younger brothers he thus had. Then they all started to go around the entire island, this earth, and all the younger brothers were killed. Thus he too failed in his mission. The work his father had sent him to do he failed to accomplish and so Earthmaker took him back and placed him on his left side.

Then Earthmaker made a fourth being and when he finished him he called him *He-who-wears-human-heads-as-earrings*.

Finally he created the last one, *Hare*. He made his body exactly like ours. He spoke to him: "You are the last one I am going to create, so try with all your strength, *Hare*." *He-who-wears-human-heads-as-earrings* had failed, so *Hare* was created. He was to be the last one. Earthmaker had created *Hare* entirely by the force of his thoughts.

Then he spoke to *Hare* and said, *"Hare,* what I am doing you will also be able to accomplish. Try with all your power. If the evil spirits injure my creation it will not be good on earth; life will not be good. Try to overcome these evil spirits." Thus he encouraged him.

When *Hare* came to this earth he said to himself, "My brothers acted in a certain way and failed." He walked along until he came to an oval lodge. From this lodge there emerged, at the time, a young woman carrying a pail. She was going toward the river. Then *Hare* said to himself, "Now my brothers were not able to do what I am going to do." There he entered the body of the young woman in order to become a human being. There in her womb he remained and yet from there he heard the shrieks and cries of the human beings. "My father sent me to help them and here I am sitting for so long time already," he thought to himself. Shrieking and crying he heard the human beings. "Too long have I been sitting here. In the end the evil spirits will destroy the human beings completely," he thought to himself. Seven months had he been waiting when he said this. Finally when the proper time had come he entered the world through an opening. Four days after that his mother died.

He lived with his grandmother. He would only leave his lodge at night. Then he would roam all around. Whenever he walked inside the lodge, light radiated from him in all directions. As soon as daylight appeared he became quiet. Throughout the day he sat thinking of the work he was to do.

The third time he left the lodge it was sunset. He traveled over half the extent of the earth and he put an end to all the bad spirits who were doing harm. "Not again will any of these live, not again will they harm my uncles and aunts, the human beings." Just before daylight appeared he returned home and there his heart would feel good. He stayed in the lodge wrapped in thought.

On the fourth day when the sun went down he left the lodge and traveled to the very ends of the earth, killing all the bad spirits he met. At about daylight he went up to the sky and pursued all the bad spirits found there, driving them to the west and killing them. Very early in the morning he walked toward his lodge filled with pleasant thoughts. "The work for which my father sent me I have now accomplished. The life of my uncles and my aunts will now be like mine," he thought to himself as he entered the lodge.

"Well, grandmother, the work my father sent me to do I have now accomplished. He sent me to look after his creation and that I have now attended to. The life of my uncles and my aunts will from now on be like mine." "But, grandson, how can that be, how can the life of your uncles and your aunts be like yours? The world is as our father created it and it cannot be altered." "The old woman must be related to the evil spirits I have killed and that is why she does not like it," he thought. "No, grandson, our father has ordained that my body, the earth shall fall in two. He ordained death lest there be a shortage of food on this earth because of surplus of people; he ordained death lest people crowd each other too much on this earth. He has therefore arranged a place for people to go to when they die."

Hare did not like it. "Surely grandmother is angry because she was related to these spirits. She is taking the part of the evil spirits." Thus he thought. "No, grandson, that is not so. At present your heart feels sore. Your uncles and aunts, however, will obtain ample life, they will live to a normal old age." So she spoke to him. "Now, grandson, get up. Your uncles and aunts will follow you in this. Try to do what I am now going to tell you. Be a man and do not look back after you have started with me."

Then they traveled around the earth. "I wonder why grandmother told me not to turn back," he thought to himself. So he looked back just the least little bit; just the least little bit he turned to the left. Immediately the place from which he had started caved in. "Oh my! Oh my! A man I thought you were, a person of prominence, and I encouraged you so much! Now, grandson, decay and death can in no way be taken back."

Around the earth they went, to the edge of the fire that stretches on each side of the earth. They united these two lines of fire so that human beings might attain old age.

"To look back she forbade me. But I have already made up my mind as to the immortality of my uncles and my aunts. When they become like me then only will I be happy. Such is my thought."

Then he went out and walked to the lodge of the spirit who lives in the east where the sun rises. Opposite him he sat down. "Well, *Hare,* there is nothing I can do for you. If the spirit ahead of me has anything he wishes to tell you, undoubtedly he will do so." Then *Hare* greeted him and went out.

He traveled toward the west. Even then he had no other thought in his head except that he would succeed. When he arrived at the lodge of the second spirit, the latter spoke to him and said, *"Hare,* what you have come for I know, but if the spirits ahead of me could say nothing how can I, the least of all of them, do so?"

Then *Hare* greeted him and left. He started for his home and arrived there crying, "My aunts and uncles must not die, they must not die!" And then he thought, "To all things death will come." He cast his thoughts upon the precipices, and they began to crumble and cave in. He cast his thoughts upon the rocks, and they began to crumble. Under the earth he cast his thoughts, and all the beings that were living there stopped moving and their limbs stiffened in death. Up above he cast his thoughts and the birds fell down dead.

Then after he had entered his lodge he took his blanket and, wrapping himself in it, he lay down crying. "Not the entire earth will suffice us when we die and in some places there will not even be enough room!"

After a while the news reached our father. He heard the human beings saying that the evil spirits would now try to utterly destroy them. The news reached him that *Hare* was not feeling well. Then Earthmaker said to the first man he had created, "*Hare* is not feeling well. Go after him." *Foolish-one* came to the earth. "*Hare,* I have come to fetch you," he said. But *Hare* did not even answer him; he did not even move in his blanket. So *Foolish-one* returned to Earthmaker. Then Earthmaker sent the second one, *Turtle,* and told him, "Do you go now after *Hare* and bring him here. Try very hard to accomplish it for he is not feeling very well." When *Turtle* came to *Hare* he told him, "*Hare,* I have come to take you back with me." But *Hare* did not even answer. Then he returned and said that *Hare* would not even answer.

Finally Earthmaker sent the fourth one he had created and said, "You are to go for *Hare* and bring him back here. Try with all your strength to accomplish this." "No matter how difficult it is I will accomplish it," he said. He reached the earth and said to *Hare,* "Indeed, for a long time has your heart been sad, *Hare.* Come, let us go home now. Get up!" Then he took him back to Earthmaker. He did not, however, take him to Earthmaker's lodge but to the one opposite, where the chief of the Thunderbirds lived. They placed him near the chief. In front of this lodge there was a mound and also a little war club painted red on one side. Thunderbird chief took the little war club and holding it lightly shook it gently. So great, however, was the noise that it made that *Hare* got frightened and almost

The Medicine Dance

ran out. Then they freed him from the sorrowful thoughts that he had had on earth and restored his spirits.

Soon after that he was taken to Earthmaker. When he came there Earthmaker said, "*Hare*, your heart must have been very sad. Full of sorrow, indeed, must your heart have been for your uncles and your aunts. Now that their lives may be benefited, a holy teaching you are to take back to them. Come, look at this!" There the sky was parted and below on earth toward the south, a long lodge stood revealed. He gazed upon it and as he looked he saw old people with very white hair. "Thus your uncles and aunts are going to be. They will make very much noise in this ceremony. Now look down again! Some help is to be given them. Not one bad spirit will I put there." Then Earthmaker pointed toward the earth again and said, "You are to go back to the earth and put this ceremony before them. Not alone are you to do it but with the aid of your own friends, *Foolish-one, Turtle, Bladder,* and *He-who-wears-human-heads-as-earrings*. Your grandmother, the Earth, will help you too. If one of your uncles and aunts performs the ceremony properly he will have more than one life. I shall always keep the door through which he may return to earth open to him. When he becomes reincarnated he can live wherever he wishes. He can return to the earth as a human being, or join the various bands of spirits, or finally become an animal under earth." Now all this Earthmaker did for us.

Then *Hare* returned to the earth and to his grandmother. "What I have tried to obtain for my uncles and my aunts, that now I have brought back with me," he said. "Grandson, how is it possible to make them immortal as ourselves? As the world was created so it must remain." "Grandmother, I say that my uncles and aunts will choose their lives for themselves, and, grandmother, you are to help me." "Good, grandson, that I will do," said grandmother thanking him.

"When the time comes my friend *Foolish-one* will come," he thought. Then *Hare* struck the drum and started his songs. All of a sudden *Foolish-one* came in. "I thought of your coming, *Foolish-one*, and you are here." "Indeed, my friend, I knew your thoughts and that is why I came." Then they went out together and outside the village they sat down to discuss what they were to do. When they returned to the lodge *Hare* thought, "My friend, *Turtle*, will come." Then *Turtle* immediately appeared. Said *Hare*, "I thought of your coming and you are here." "Yes, my friend, I knew your thoughts and that is why I came." In the same way *Bladder* came. Finally *Hare* fixed his thoughts on *He-who-wears-human-heads-as-earrings* and he came.

Grandmother listened to them very quietly but she could not understand what they were saying. Then after a while *Hare said*, "What I tried to obtain for my uncles and my aunts I have accomplished. You are now going to hear what it is. Come near the fireplace and sit down and then you will hear about it. I know that you too, grandmother, will be anxious to help the human beings." "Indeed, grandson, I am." She got up, took her handiwork, sat down near the five of them and laid her hands upon their head. She placed her work in front of her grandson, *Hare*. Then she spoke and said, "If you get this ceremony, the Medicine Dance, for your uncles and your aunts, they will live happily. Forever are they to do this." Then she asked, "Grandson, what is the nature of the work that I am to do for you? Well, this is it. Now look at me. Earth-maker, our father, had me bring the following things for your uncles and your aunts. I am going to give them that with which they can always obtain life." Then she opened her dress and there where the heart is, on the left, green leaves became visible and a stalk like an ear. The stalk was white as a blossom. It was corn. "For your uncles and aunts, Earthmaker, our father has permitted me to bring corn." Thus did a stalk become visible whose leaves were very green and whose tassels were very white.

Then the five of them arose and said, "Let us greet our grandmother." So they walked up to her and laid their hands upon her head. "It is good, grandmother," said *Hare*. "This is what I meant when I said you were to help the human beings."

Then *Hare* went out and when he got to a place in the east he stopped. Then he turned to the west. Then he thought, "This is the way it will be." He took eight yellow female snakes and threw them in the air. As they fell they became transformed into the side-poles of the lodge. He turned their heads toward the east and their tails toward the west. He used rattlesnakes to tie them with. The doorway he made of two snakes, a black female snake on the left and a male snake on the right. The doors at the rear end of the lodge he made of blue female snakes. Then he took some reed-grass and threw it over the lodge so that it was completely covered. He took another piece of reed-grass and threw it inside the lodge where it became the white mats on which we stand. A bearskin hide he threw in on the right side and it extended along the whole length of the lodge. On the other side he threw a deerskin hide. Then he made a door of a real living mountain lion. This he did in order to prevent any bad spirits from entering. At the west door he placed a buffalo bull. When he had completed all these things, he looked inside the lodge and there he heard these animals bellowing and roaring at each other. Light radiated all over the lodge.

He now started for the lodge, he first and his friends following. "Well, my friends, I am through; the lodge is finished. Grandmother, stand up and come with us!" She walked first and after her they all came. When they arrived at the door, the fear-inspiring lion snapped his teeth. But they entered and walked around the lodge until they came to the place where they had first come in. Then *Hare* sent a number of public criers, a bear and a wolf, to traverse the entire length of the earth and invite the spirits to the ceremony. Along with them were also sent winged messengers, the crow and the swan.

When these started they all looked young but when they returned their bodies had become old and devoid of hair and they had to support themselves on staffs. The birds too when they returned, came back with wings exhausted, with eyebrows hanging over their eyes, looking very old indeed. In front of *Hare's* seat they stopped and said to him, "Your uncles and aunts, when they speak of you, will forever praise you. We have placed many life-giving objects within this lodge." "Well, my friends," said *Hare,* "it is good. This is what I wanted. I thank you in the names of my uncles and aunts."

Then all the messengers who had been sent out returned. The first four beings created by Earthmaker also came. They stood at the door ready to enter. The oldest one started but turned back frightened by the animals he saw within. The next two also tried but recoiled back afraid. Finally the youngest opened the door and led them in. They made the circuit of the lodge and at the door *Hare* took the eldest and placed him in the seat at the east. Then he walked around and placed the next one at the north, then one at the west and one at the south. Then *Hare* took his own seat.

Now the various spirits who had been invited began to enter. Then came the human beings, those of the bird clan, of the bear clan, the wolf clan, the snake clan, etc. Last came the one they were to initiate.

Then *Hare* rose and spoke, "My friends, I have had you come together because my uncles and aunts had been living a very pitiable life. You are to teach them the life they are to live and which is to be handed down from one generation to the other. That is what I ask of you. You have now heard what it is I want. I leave everything else to be done and said by those in the east."

Then the one in the east seat arose and said, "We are to teach our friends, the uncles and aunts of *Hare,* the meaning of life. This they may hand down from generation to generation. To-day for the first time has this thing been discussed. All that life consists of—wealth, honor and happiness—they shall have from now on." The other three spirits, the one in the north, the west, and the south, all said the same thing. When they finished each one returned to his own seat.

Now *Hare* got up again and said, "This is what I desired for my uncles and aunts. This lodge I made for them and as long as they follow the precepts taught in this lodge of creation, they will be invulnerable. For that reason have these seats been made for them, that whosoever so desires may sit therein."

All day long the spirits taught the one who was to be initiated and when the sun was on the treetops and when it was time to stop, the spirits dispersed. As they left they took with them half of the light that had been radiated in the lodge. As they went out they rubbed against the door-posts. They pushed these deep into the ground so that they would not fall over.

Hare now rose and spoke again, "Grandmother, I shall ever be sitting ready for any of my uncles and aunts who will perform this ceremony that has been taught them. With tears my uncles and aunts will come to me and my heart will ache for them. I will go above and sit down, and if any person performs this ceremony, then he will become as I am. Now look at me, grandmother, look at my body!" The old woman looked and behold! he had become a small boy. "Grandmother," said *Hare,* "if any one repeats this ceremony properly, he will become just like this. Now look at me again," *Hare* said. She looked at him and he had become a full-grown man. When she looked for the third time he had become middle-aged, his hair was interspersed with gray. When she looked for the fourth time, his head was covered as if he were wearing a swan as a headdress and he leaned tremblingly on his staff, standing in the east. "Well, grandmother," said *Hare,* "if any of my uncles perform this ceremony properly this is the way they will live."

"It is good, grandson," said the old woman. "However not only your uncles will live like that if they perform the ceremony properly. The same will apply to your aunts. Now look at me, grandson." *Hare* looked and there stood a very young woman, her hair like a smooth shawl. "It is good," said *Hare;* "in the name of my aunts I thank you." Then again he was asked to look and he saw a woman in middle age, her hair almost gray. When he looked the fourth time, her hair was entirely dried up, there was a hollow in the nape of her neck, her chin protruded trembling, like a wooden poker burnt short, and her whole appearance was that of duck looking at the sun.

The Medicine Dance

'Well, grandmother, this is what I meant when I said that you were to help me. My uncles and aunts have now received all that I desired for them. I thank you."

Now throughout the ceremony I felt all the time that we were merely deceiving the spectators. When it was all over the members of my band told me that in two years I would be able to imitate the sounds of animals to my heart's content for I had taken the place of a great medicine man. Those who have the privilege of dancing obtain it by making gifts to the older members and thus buying the right. Those who do not buy this right or are not given permission to use it, are not allowed to dance. It is the same way with the shooting. Unless, for instance, a man buys the right, he is not allowed to extend his arms at full length when he shoots, but he must hold them close to his breast. The right to drum as well as the right to shake the gourd rattles, all these things must be bought. In fact, almost everything must be bought. I was told, however, that I would not have to go through all this training but would become a great medicine man immediately. That pleased me. I was given a gray squirrel-skin to use as a medicine pouch and I was told that it was really alive and that I had the power to make it cry aloud. I had seen people doing this and I had always envied them. This was another of the things I was anxious to do. Indeed I wondered greatly how it could be done. When the dance was over my father went away and left me at that place alone. He left me at the home of the deceased person's wife. I did not go back to school but, instead, stayed near the old woman and did various jobs for her. There I stayed all spring.

I had been told that if a person initiated into the Medicine Dance did not regard the affair as sacred this was a sign that he would die soon. This frightened me a good deal for I had been thinking of the whole matter in a very light-hearted fashion and I now felt that this was an indication that I would soon die. I did my best therefore to consider it a sacred ceremony. In spite of all this, however, I did not succeed.

About this time I left for Tomah. It was about the middle of the summer. I stayed and lived with my grandfather and from that time on was taught by him many of the details of the Medicine Dance. For instance, when I prepared a sweat-bath for him he would teach me some of the songs. I accordingly prepared the bath for him frequently. He would always be grateful and that is another of the reasons why I was glad to do it. Before long I had learned all the songs he knew so that when I was invited to a Medicine Dance I would do all the singing and he would only do the talking. From that time on I said that it was a sacred affair, and from then on I participated in the ceremony for the greatness inhering in it. I boasted of its greatness in the presence of women, in order to make a good impression upon them.

§15. *Marriage*

About this time I joined a show and danced. I was always very fond of dancing and now I got a chance to go around and dance all the time and even got paid for it. I had money all the time. The people with whom I went around never saved anything and were always without funds, for they spent all their money on drink. I, however, never drank. After a while I got into the habit of going with these shows every fall.

One fall I did not go and, instead, stayed with my grandfather. He told me to get married. I was about twenty-three years old then. I had courted women ever since I was old enough to do so. Every time I did anything I always thought of women in connection with it. I tried to court as many as I could. I wanted badly to be a beau, for I considered it a great thing. I wanted to be a ladies' man.

My grandfather had wanted me to marry a certain girl so I went over to the place where she was staying. When I arrived there I tried to meet the girl secretly and succeeded in doing so. I told her of my intention of marrying her and asked her to go home with me. Then she went back, for I had met her some distance from her home.

After a short time she came back all dressed up and

ready. She had on a waist covered with silver buckles and a beautifully colored hair ornament; she wore many strings of beads around her neck and had bracelets around her wrists. Her fingers were covered with rings. She wore a pair of ornamented leggings and ornamented moccasins with wide flaps. In each ear she had about a half dozen ear-holes and they were full of small silver pieces made into ear ornaments. She was painted, her cheeks red, and the parting of her hair red. She was all dressed up.

I came to her on horseback. Then we rode together. We were not going to return to the place from which I had started that night, because I had been previously asked to sing at a Medicine Feast at a place on our way home. On the way I therefore hid the girl near the place where the feast was to be given.

The girl had a red blanket, and I hid her under a small oak bush. Unfortunately it rained all that night and the next morning, and when, early in the morning, I went to where I had hidden the girl I found her still there, but soaked through and through from the rain. Her paint was smeared all over her face in such a way that she could hardly be recognized. When we arrived home my grandfather's wife came out to meet us. She helped the girl down from the horse and took her into the lodge. Then we ate and when we were through the girl took off her clothing and gave it to my grandparents who in return gave her other clothing. After the girl had stayed there three nights she had her menses and had to go to her special lodge and sleep

Marriage

there. Shortly after a horse was given to this girl I had married.

Some time after, my grandfather had a private talk with me and he said, "Grandson, it is said that this girl you have married is not a virgin and I am not pleased with it, as this is your first marriage and you are a young man. I suppose you know whether this is true or not, whether or not she is a maiden?" "Yes," I answered, "I know." "Well, you do not have to live with her then if you don't care to," he said. So I went away on a visit and from there I went home for good. After some time I learned that she also had gone back to her home. My grandfather was glad that I had not stayed with her and he told me, "You can marry another and a better one, one that I shall choose for you." However I said to him, "Grandfather, you have begged women for me often enough. Don't ever do it again for I don't care to marry a woman who has to be begged for." He was not at all pleased at this for he said that I was not allowing him to tell me what to do.

§16. *Shows*

About this time we went to the Sioux country on a visit. There were a number of us. While there I was adopted as a friend and given a pony. When I returned to my home I used to ride around on my pony. That fall a number of Winnebago were going to join a show and I decided to go along with them. I was a good dancer. We went to all the large cities of the country.

With us there were two grass widows and after a while I used to go with one of them secretly. This woman used to drink beer. Soon I began to go with the other woman also. They both drank a good deal and often asked me to drink with them, but I always refused. I finally married one of these women, although I continued frequenting the other one at the same time. We lived in a tipi. As I said, they both drank beer and gradually I got to drinking it too. Soon I drank a great deal and began to like it. I kept this a secret from my people and told the women to do the same. Finally, however, as I began drinking frequently, a friend of mine found out about it and then the two of us used to drink together. Then the owner of the show discovered that I was drinking. He thought a good deal of me, that my dancing was better than that of the others, and when he learned that

I was drinking, he told me that he would treat me and the two women to beer that very night. I drank a lot of it that night and I enjoyed it immensely. After that, of course, I was not able to keep the fact of my drinking from other people. I talked at the top of my voice under the influence of liquor and was very happy. Every few minutes I would suddenly begin to sing out loudly. Then I began drinking whisky in addition to beer, and got drunk. On the following morning I said I would never do it again, but in a short time I was drinking beer again secretly.

Eventually the show was over and we all went to our homes. We had to go across Lake Michigan. It was very stormy and we all got sick. Then my friend said, "Say, let us drink so that we may not be sick." He took out some whisky which he was carrying in a flask and we drank all night. Very early in the morning we got to Milwaukee. There we ate our breakfast and continued on our way home, to Black River Falls. We drank all the way on the train and when we reached our destination we were still drinking. All my relatives saw that I was drunk. They were very sorry and an older sister of mine wept when she saw me. I there made up my mind that I would never do it again. At about that time we received our annuity payment and although I had money I did not drink any more for some time.

After we had spent what we had received in annuities the hunting season began. I went along with the others to the hunting grounds. I ran away from the two women with whom I had been living. We spent some time hunting. Every morning we would get up very early, stay out the whole day and not return until the night. Often although we had been on our feet all day we would not find time to have our noon meal. At night, regularly, we would take our sweat-baths. We took these sweat-baths because they are supposed to act as magical charms to ensure success in hunting. It was always very refreshing to take them and then plunge into cold water, whether at night or in the morning.

§17. *A Woman Bewitches Me*

Once when I returned to the camp I found some other people there. There I also found my grandfather. He had brought along with him one of the two women with whom I had been living, the older one. I did not like it at all. My grandfather asked me to live with her and I did so during the hunting season. When it was over this woman remained there and I returned to my home with another one. My former wife stayed there a long time, but when she got tired of waiting for me to return, she left.

Just about this time I heard that this former wife of mine, before going away, had used some magical medicine on me. A medicine feast was immediately given me and my scalp treated to counteract the evil effect of what she had used. It was said that she had taken one of my hairs and dipped it into her medicine bundle. This she did in order to prevent me from ever leaving her. If then I left her I would suffer from a headache and perhaps even die. Such was the belief. Fortunately the matter was discovered, my scalp treated and the hair she had taken recovered and washed with medicine. Nothing therefore happened to me.

From that time on I began to live with as many women as I could, for I had developed the idea that I was a lady-killer.

§18. *My Brother Is Murdered*

Shortly after this my elder brother was killed. We two had grown up together and had hardly ever been separated. I felt quite heartbroken over it. I longed to kill the man who had murdered him. I felt that it would be better if I myself were dead. In this frame of mind I took to drinking a great deal. Indeed it was my wish to die drinking and I would announce this when I was drinking heavily. Up to that time I had drunk secretly, but now I did so openly. Soon I became a confirmed drunkard. By that time I had quite forgotten the fact that I had wanted to die. Indeed I enjoyed drinking very much.

I got into the habit, then, of giving women whisky and getting them hopelessly drunk and then I would steal anything of value they possessed. I also learned to box and soon became quite expert. I was never defeated, and in consequence treated every one roughly. Every one was afraid of me because of my skill with the gloves. My father was a strong man and so were my elder brothers, and neither of them had ever been defeated at wrestling. For all these reasons I was very arrogant. Besides all this I was very tall. I am six feet two inches high and weigh about two hundred and fifty pounds. In actual fact I was not really as strong as I pretended for whenever I woke up from a drunken orgy I found myself firmly bound.

All I did was to wander from place to place, from one woman to another. I had four sisters and from them and from my parents did I receive all that I possessed and yet in spite of this, I claimed to be a great man! I then had two women staying with me as my wives. At one time I had as many as four, two at my parents' house and two at certain relatives of mine. I wasn't serious with any one of them. I lied all the time; I was always telling falsehoods. On one occasion I had four children born to me and each one had a different mother. Even after that I continued courting women and drinking.

In the spring there was always work to do. We rolled logs down the stream and drank. I accepted such occupations because I could then always get as much drink as I wanted. Whenever I had any money I spent it on getting some woman drunk.

§19. *The Effect of a Pretended Blessing*

I was now drinking heavily all the time and I began to boast of being a holy man. I claimed that I had been blessed by certain spirits and I made this claim again and again. Of course this was all a lie, for I had never felt a stirring of any kind within me. I made the claim because I had heard others doing it. Generally I made this claim when I was just about drunk, just on the verge of getting boisterous but still vaguely conscious of what I was saying. Then I would say, for instance, that I had been blessed by a Grizzly-spirit, that he had blessed me with the power of being uncontrollable, that he had taught me certain songs. These I would then sing at the top of my voice. I used to exert all the power I had to imitate a grizzly bear. The bystanders would try to hold me but it always required a large number of men to do so. Now I thought this exhibition of mine an act worthy of praise.

After that I began to claim that I had been blessed by many spirits. I made the claim at one time that I was really the reincarnation of one of the benevolent giant spirits and that my name was *Good-heart*, that I was now living as a human being among men. Such was my claim and people believed me.

Once when I was on one of my drinking sprees I

visited the lodge of a relative of mine. There I found a woman whom I had the right to call niece and whom I could therefore tease. Just in jest I used to call her "mother" and "sister." Now on this particular occasion after food had been offered me, I began teasing her as usual when one of the women sitting around there said, "My younger brother, your niece is really in a condition to excite your compassion and not to fool with. She is in fact about to face death, for she is going to be confined soon and she generally manages barely to escape death then." "Oh, is that so?" answered I. "Well, elder sister, this time my niece is not going to suffer. Up above, in the heavens, there exist four women, sisters, and these blessed me, telling me that if I ever called upon them for help they would help me. Now to these I shall offer tobacco and when my niece is about to be delivered, she, too, must ask for help." Thus I spoke to her. The woman thanked me. I had told a terrible falsehood. I said all this because I was very hungry and I knew that I would then receive enough to appease my hunger. I had nothing else to say.

Some time after this I saw the women in town. The older woman ran over to me and said, "My younger brother, all is well. Your niece is in wonderful condition; she is very well indeed. She has just given birth to a child and within three days of its birth she was able to chop wood. Never before has such a thing happened to her. It is good. As soon as the annuity payment is made you may have the child's portion for drink." Thus she spoke. I was surprised. Perhaps I am really holy, after all, I thought.

After this incident, of course, I boasted of my powers even more, for now I was really convinced that I possessed sacred power. I talked as do those who have knowledge of blessings obtained from all the spirits in creation; I spoke with all the authority of a great medicine man. I used to do the singing for my band during the performance of the Medicine Dance, and as I had a deep bass voice, everybody liked it. Sometimes I would be given offerings of food in a kettle.

I always drank a great deal whenever a Medicine Dance was given and frequently I would knock people unconscious when I was drunk, even those in the vicinity of the camp.

§20. *I Have a Fight*

Once we went out hunting game in the fall of the
year. We used to sell the hindquarters and sometimes ship them as far as Chicago. We were of course
only permitted to hunt for thirty days. The law was
that if any one hunted longer than that he would be
arrested. Yet in spite of all we hunted for a longer
time because we felt that the law was meant only for
the Whites. One day, however, in shipping deer away,
we were detected. One of my brothers and myself
were arrested, taken to court and convicted. We had
to spend sixty days in jail. During my imprisonment
I never had my hair cut and from that time on, I always wore it long. I told the people that a spirit called
Foolish-one [24] had instructed me to do this and that he
had blessed me. I also told my older brother, the one
who was still living, to do the same thing and that if he,
too, let his hair grow, *Foolish-one* would bless him with
long life. From that time on I wore long hair.

After that I joined a show of the Whites. People
liked me very much on account of my long hair and I
was well paid. I kept on drinking all the time. I there
learned to ride a bicycle and mount and ride wild

[24] The clown of Winnebago mythology. He is, however, regarded
as having some of the characteristics of a spirit and, very occasionally, blessing an individual.

[139]

horses. I used to call myself a cowboy, principally because I wore my hair long. Many vicious horses did I ride, and I was thrown off many times. I did all this not because I felt myself to be an expert, but because I was wild. On one occasion I took part in a bicycle race on a regular racetrack. I was in full Indian costume and wore long hair.

The show I had joined played at St. Paul. I took part in it every summer. I became acquainted with many people and so I was asked to come again every year. Finally it got so that I would not even return to the Indians in winter.

One season some one asked me to collect a number of Indians of whom I was to be in charge. I was told that I would be allowed ten dollars a week for each Indian and that I could pay them whatever I liked. I was quite satisfied, for I could pay them five dollars a week and thus make some money, I thought. I therefore persuaded a number of people to go along with me and we all started. We rode to the place where we were to meet the man who had made the arrangements. From there we started out and went from fair to fair. We never made any money, however, and went bankrupt. The man could not even pay us. We felt very angry and we then went to another show with whose manager I was acquainted. We were to divide the receipts.

Once we were to give our show at a certain place for the last time, for the cold weather was setting in. It was thus our last day. One of the boys came to me and told me that some one had struck him. I got angry and told him to point out the person who had done it. Just then the very person appeared and I tried to strike him, but he got away. I succeeded, however, in striking him with a drumstick. That evening I was told that the man whom I had struck had said that he was going to kill a certain Indian. "Perhaps he doesn't know that he also is subject to death," I answered. "Indeed, I am anxious to get ahold of him." After the show was finished we put on our civilian clothes and took our handbags. "None of you must go out alone," I warned them, "for you might get hurt." One of my boys was on horseback and was taking his horse to water it at a trough. His pony was taken away from him and he returned without it. His hat, too, had been stolen. Indeed he barely escaped with his life. "Come, let us go back," I said. I told the other boys to go right on and not to worry about me. I gave them my handbag and then returned to the place where the first boy had been attacked. Before we got there the same boy was attacked and set upon with clubs. We were right in the midst of a big crowd of Whites. These shouted and chased him. When they saw me they started for me. I fought them with my bare fists, turning from side to side. I was completely surrounded by them. Whenever any one got near enough to me I struck him. Then I started to run and was hit on the head, but I was not knocked unconscious. I was now angry and I struck out at all within reach. If I had had a weapon

I would have killed some of them. Several now fell upon me and I was struck on the head until it was entirely covered with blood. I started for the show tents which had not yet been taken down. Just then the man who had begun all the trouble came toward me with a hatchet. I went for him and when he raised the hatchet I struck him and knocked him down, for I hit him straight in the mouth.

A policeman now came forward and led me to our show tents. I was covered with blood. The women were weeping and told the policeman who I was, that it was not my fault and that I had not been drinking. I was taken to jail. I told the policeman that we ought not to be locked up for we had not started the trouble. The others ought to be locked up, we said, for it was the particular man who had hit my boy who had been drinking. "You are right," said the policeman. "I will go back and look for your things. Yet you ought not to be on the street for you have hurt many people. You had better stay in jail for a few hours for many people are on the watch for you. Now I'll go for your pony and then you can do what you like." They put me in jail and there I found the Indian about whom all the trouble had started. "Well, this is good," he said. "I thought they had killed you. Well, how many did you kill?" "I didn't kill any one," I answered. "It is good, for I thought they had either killed you or that you had killed them."

Then I washed the blood from my head. Soon after the policeman returned and brought my pony with him, as well as my hat. Then he said, "You are to go home immediately. It is true that you have been dealt with unfairly, but this is a regular fair town, and if any trouble starts in the courts about this affair, it will hurt our fairs in the future. We shall therefore not go to law about it. The man who started the trouble is the owner of a large hotel, and in addition, owns a trotting horse. You have knocked out all the teeth of this hotel-keeper, and we do not know whether he will live or not. You have bruised other people, too, badly. So you had better go home."

From there we started for our home. My partner rode a pony and rode through the middle of the town on it. I went in the same direction. He was afraid to go through the crowd of white people. A policeman escorted us out to the edge of the town. There we told him that we wanted some whisky and he went into a saloon and bought us two quarts. We both started then, sitting on a small two-year-old pony that belonged to my partner. Every time a team drove by we got frightened. After we had been drinking a little, however, we said that if the fight were to occur again, we would surely kill some one for we were sorry about the way in which it had ended. No one pursued us, however.

There were some Indians living in the neighborhood and we used to go to visit them every night. When I told them about what had happened they got quite frightened for they thought these white people would come out there to fight. So they moved away on the following morning. The other man and I took up their trail and followed. We still rode the little pony together. We had plenty of whisky with us. At night we came upon their camps. These poor people were really trying to get away from us for they thought that the white people would really follow us and fight.

There I found out that my relatives were camping nearby, so I went over to see them. They felt very sorry for us when we told them what had happened. They were working at the time, digging potatoes. I stayed with them at the house of a certain woman.

§21. *Dissipation*

While staying at this woman's lodge I was one day handed a paper by a woman, in which she told me that she was married, that she was living at a certain place, and that if I came over, she would do whatever I said. I told the woman with whom I was living about it, and she said, "Go after her, that I may have her as my companion." Her father had a horse, and on it I rode over to the woman's house. I went there secretly, and watched the people digging potatoes, for their camp was nearby. The man to whom this woman was married was also living with another woman at the same time. The woman I was after was staying in this camp. I approached her secretly and when I reached the place she got herself ready to go with me. The two of us rode on a pony, and it so happened that we had to pass the place where the husband was working. He pursued us, but we managed to get away. In a short time I arrived home, and my wife received the second woman willingly. They would sleep with me on alternate nights.

After we finished our work there, we went to the place from which we had originally come, and we arrived home just in time for the annuity payment. The superintendent of the Wittenberg school made the payment. At about the same time, one of the two women with whom I was living was taken away from me. She went to live with another man. When the payment was over here, the superintendent went to Necedah to pay the people there, and I went along, for I was doing what we called "chasing the payment." There, and at Red Hill, I deceived many women, and thus obtained quite a large sum of money. Then I started off with a number of other young men. By this time I was spending all my time drinking.

I got on the train at night. We were to change cars at a place called Honsa and from there we were to ride in a freight car. When we had gone only a short distance the conductor saw us and put us off. We were all drinking heavily. One man had lost his hat and was walking bareheaded. We walked along until we came to a pasture, and there we found some dry wood with which we built a fire. We had deceided to sleep there. We had plenty of whisky with us. Late at night we became thirsty and so we looked around for water. We found a number of pools scattered around, and out of these we drank. Then we went to sleep. The next morning when we woke up we saw a good well near us, but we ourselves had drunk out of the water and mud in which pigs had been wallowing.

In the morning when the train arrived we boarded it. Eventually we reached our destination, and there found many people, drinking and making a lot of noise. That was exactly the place I had been looking for. Whenever I saw a person drunk I would steal whatever he happened to have, for I had become a thief. If I saw a woman drunk, I would steal her, for I was an adulterer. What I was looking for mainly was a woman to cohabit with, for in this way, I was able to get all her money. If any woman wanted to cohabit with me, she would have to give me all the money she had. This is the sort of thing I was doing. In this way I often succeeded in inducing two or three women to live with me at the same time.

After finishing at Necedah the superintendent always went to Tomah to pay the people there, and from Tomah he would proceed to Black River Falls. At Black River Falls the last payment was made, and for that reason it was always an extremely noisy place on such an occasion. All who liked this kind of a life, all who used to chase payments for the fun of it, would be there. Marriages would get badly mixed up here, and there would always be stealing of one another's wives, fighting, robbery, etc. Even those married people who had been faithful to each other up till then, would become unfaithful. Many people would get hurt. When the last payment had been made, all those who had not spent their last cent on drink would begin gambling, the men and women playing poker. Only when our last cent was gone would we stop and settle down. Many of us were generally left without enough money to go home.

§22. *We Kill a Pottawattomie*

I never married any woman permanently. I would live with one for awhile, and then with another. Sometimes upon my return after an absence I would find my temporary wife living with another man. This is the way in which I acted.

My father had brought me up and had encouraged me to fast, so that I might be blessed by all the spirits that exist, and thus live in comfort. My father had raised me so that I should desire to obtain war honors,[25] so that I should not be like one who wears skirts. That was the reason he had me join the Medicine Dance so that people should not be able to ridicule me. My father taught me to lead a sober and sane life and my grandfather, during the time I lived with him, had told me the same. They both encouraged me to give feasts and to ask the spirits for war honors.

At that time I had a comrade, and one day he said to me, "We have been thinking of something, have we not, friend?   We ought to try and obtain some external emblem of our bravery.   Do we not always try to wear feathers at a Warrior Dance?   Well, then, let us try

[25] These war honors were the following: touching the body of a slain enemy first, killing an enemy, touching the body second, touching it third, stealing a horse. All of them entitled the possessor to wear an eagle feather in his hair.

to obtain war honors, so that we can wear head ornaments." So did we both speak to each other. We both liked the idea, and so we decided to go in search of war honors. We decided to kill a man of another tribe; we meant to perform an act of bravery. We started out finally. There were four of us, and we went to a place where other tribesmen congregated. We took the train and carried some baggage with us. We took ropes along, for we intended to steal some horses, and if we found the opportunity, kill a man. Horse stealing was regarded as a praiseworthy feat, and I had always admired the people who recounted the number of times they had stolen horses, at one of the Warrior Dances. That was why I wished to do these things.

We proceeded to a place where horses of other tribes used to pasture. Just as we got there we saw the owner of some of these horses and killed him. My friend killed him. Then we went home, and secretly I told my father all about it. I said to him, "Father, you said it was good to be a warrior and you encouraged me to fast and I did so. You encouraged me to give feasts and I did so. Now we have just returned from a trip. We were looking for war honors and the young people who were accompanying me decided that I should lead them. I told them that it was a difficult thing to lead warriors, my father had always told me, and that I had always been given to understand that a person could lead a war-party only in consequence of a specific blessing received from the spirits. I was not conscious of having received any such, I told him.

Thus I spoke. However, they made me an offering of tobacco as they asked me, and I accepted the tobacco saying that I would at least make an offering of tobacco for them. Then I offered tobacco to the Thunderbirds and asked them for rain, that we might walk in the protection and power of rain. This offering we made in the morning and it rained all that day. Then we went to the place where we knew that we could find horses. When we got there we met the owner of the horses and spoke to him. We accompanied him to a carpenter shop nearby, and there killed him. I struck his dead body, counted coup [26] first, and announced my new name, as I gave a war-whoop. I shouted '*Big-Winnebago* has counted coup on his man.' Then the others counted coup also. We searched his pockets and found medicine and money in them. The money we divided among ourselves. After that we cut out his heart, for we had heard that hearts were used for medicine. That is why we cut out his heart. He had a gun and that we took away from him and hid."

Then my father said to me, "My son, it is good. Your life is no longer an effeminate one. This is the manner in which our ancestors encouraged us to live. It is the will of the spirits in control of war that has led

[26] The first four war honors enumerated above are called "counting coup" by the Whites. *Coup* is the French for *strike* and the expression owes its origin to the custom of warriors counting the number of people they have killed or honors they have obtained by striking the post at the grave of the particular person for whose benefit they are recounting their achievements.

you to do this. Of your own initiative you could not possibly have done it. However, we had better not have a Victory Dance as yet. We have the honor anyhow. We must be careful about the Whites. In the old days we were at liberty to live in our own way, and when such a deed as yours became known, your sisters would rejoice and dance, we are told. Now, however, the law of the Whites is to be feared. In due time you will get a chance to announce your feat and then you can wear a head ornament for you have earned that right for yourself."

§23. *I Take a Trip to Nebraska*

Shortly after this I had to go to Nebraska. It was in connection with a child I once had, a boy who had died when he was two years old. His mother's father then adopted another one in his place. This child belonged to the Menominee tribe. I had to go there for I was the adopted father of the child and he was thus my son, the one who was taking my dead son's place. I gave the boy a horse at the ceremony performed to fill the dead child's place. The ceremony itself was the Sore Eye Dance.[27] The relatives of the mother gave me some beaded bags, two boxes of maple sugar, etc. Before I had started out for Nebraska, when I was still living in Wittenberg, the boy came to me. I was then living with a woman, and she gave me many things that I was to take along with me to Nebraska and for which she hoped I would get horses in return.

When I started, I stopped at Black River Falls. I went to a woman with whom I had once lived, in order to take her along with me, but she refused. I had gone

[27] The Sore Eye Dance, called more correctly the Society-of-those-who-have-been-blessed-by-the-Night-Spirits, is a secret society organized something like that of the Medicine Dance but quite different in object. It is primarily a war ceremony and its nickname of Sore Eye Dance arose out of the fact that it was so frequently given after the return of a successful war party that the people attending it, got sore eyes from staying up so long.

to see her when I was drinking heavily. I therefore had to go on alone. I had my gun with me. I arrived at Nebraska in midsummer. I arrived there very early in the morning, and there I met a man whom I had once known, a person who used to go around a good deal. There were many people present. We sat somewhat on one side, and he and his wife drank with me. I told him what I had done, how I had counted coup on a Pottawattomie, and he shook hands and said that he too had counted coup and that he was going to wear a head ornament. Then they took me to the place where they lived, carrying all my things for me.

The next day the Nebraska Winnebago were going to celebrate. There was to be a general gathering for a week. The people with whom I was staying joined the others at the gathering. At the gathering itself I met two men whom I knew and who recognized me. They shook hands with me. They were riding in a buggy, and when they left, they took me along. On the road they stopped, and we got out of the buggy and began drinking out of a jug containing four quarts of whisky which we had along with us. I joined them in the drinks. We then went back to the gathering, where I met an uncle of mine. To him I presented my gun, and he was delighted.

The gathering itself was a very large one, and we danced every day. I also prepared myself and took part in the dance and gave away many things. I received in return two ponies, a harness, and a top-buggy. I remained there for some time after the celebration was over. Indeed, I even got married there. I kept on drinking all the time. It was then that a nephew of mine begged me to give him my buggy. A nephew has the privilege of asking his uncle for anything, and the uncle must give it. In return the uncle can compel the nephew to work for him at any time.

Some time after that I went to visit an uncle of mine. He said, "Nephew, to-morrow they are going to have a Medicine Dance, and to-night they are going to have a trial performance.[28] Your aunt is going to buy provisions for the meal, and you may go along with her." So I went along. When we got to town we drank, and on the following day it was rumored that the woman and myself were missing. The buggy in which we were riding was quite broken, my hat was gone, and my trousers ripped open. I immediately went back to the place I had come from, even though the Medicine Dance was being given. The woman, I heard, was still missing. I then went to the place at which I had been staying, and remained there all day. I got very tired. In the morning I mounted a horse and went to town. There I was arrested. I was asked what I was doing in the town. "I am not doing anything; I am merely visiting around." Then the one in charge of the law said that I was to pay ten dollars and that if I did not do so, he would send me to prison. I therefore sold my horse for twenty dollars, and out of it I paid the ten

[28] The first part of the regular Medicine Dance is supposed to be merely a rehearsal for the following day when the main ceremony is given and is in consequence called the "trial" performance.

dollars. It was a good horse. Then the lawyer said, "You have committed many crimes, and you had better go to the place from which you came. If you stay here any longer, we will lock you up."

I left that same day. Two old men were going to Wisconsin, and I went with them. They did not know how to speak English, so they took me as their interpreter. I left one of my horses in the pasture there. These men were very fond of whisky, and I bought whisky for them all along the route. After a time we arrived in Wisconsin, just at the cranberry-picking season. I was drunk when we reached our destination. As we approached my home I told the old men that they should come and visit me. As I said it, I gave a whoop.

§ 24. *A Woman Quarrels with Me*

I was met by my father and mother and a woman who was living with me before I left. They were very glad to see me. When I got home I found many people camping there. At the camp the woman fixed a bed for me, gave me some food, and told me to lie down with her. Instead, I went out and made inquiries about a woman with whom I had once lived. I found that she was still there. To her lodge I went, and with her I stayed that night. In the morning the other woman was angry. However, I continued staying with this new one. Late on the following night some one woke me up. "Come out," the voice said. I went out with a blanket around me and found my former wife. She it was who was calling me. She said, "In the morning the annuity payment is to be paid in Necedah. I am going there to-night, and I want you to go with me." "I haven't any money," I answered. "As though you ever had any money of your own when you wanted to do something!" I refused to go with her. She persisted, and finally I went back and lay down. After a while she followed me inside and hit me very hard and called me names. She kicked me and pulled my hair. "If I had anything with which to kill you, I would kill you." Finally I got angry, and she stopped and went away.

§25. *I Get Delirium Tremens*

During the cranberry-picking season I drank all the time, and after that chased the payments. I continued drinking. When the payments had all been made, I went to Black River Falls. I was entirely without money. I was supposed to go back to Wittenberg, but I didn't have the fare. I went back to the Indians and stayed all night. In the morning I was sick. I was shaking from head to foot. When I tried to drink coffee, I would spill it; when I lay down, I used to see big snakes. I cried out and got up. Then when I wanted to go to sleep again, I thought I heard some one calling me. I raised the cover of my bed and looked around, but saw nothing. Whenever the wind blew, I thought I heard singing. I thought I heard imaginary people spit very loudly; I heard them and I could not sleep. As soon as I closed my eyes I began to see things. I saw things that were happening in a distant country. I saw ghosts on horseback, drunk. Five or six of them were on one horse, and they were singing. I recognized them, for they were people who had died long before. I heard the words of their song as they sang:

"I, even I, must die some time, so of what value is anything, I think."

Thus they sang, and it made a good song. I myself learned it, and later on it became a drinking song known by many people. I like it very much.

The next morning I rode on a train, and after a while we came to a town. Two days after this I stopped drinking and kept it up throughout the whole winter because I was unable to drink. I vomited every time I tried to drink beer. Throughout the winter I did not drink, and I kept this up until the following summer.

§26. *I Am Arrested for Murder and Confess*

Two years elapsed. At about that time we heard that the men who were responsible for the disappearance of the Pottawattomie had been discovered. One of those who had taken part in his murder had been to Nebraska and had there announced his deed in recounting his acts of bravery at a Warrior Dance. Such was the rumor. This same man had also announced it at a funeral wake. It was in this way that the facts had come out.

That same winter, while I was living in the forest cutting wood, two men came to me one night. They were officers. They mentioned a man's name to me and asked me if I knew him. I said, "Yes." "Well," said they, "let us go to town. We want to ask you some things." They told me to get ready. I did so and rode in a wagon they possessed. Then the men asked me, "Did Peter kill this man? Do you know?" "I do not know," I said to them. Then they told me from what source they had obtained the information and again asked me, "Did you ever hear anything about it?" "No," I answered. "Did you know that this man was missing?" "I did hear that a man had been missing, but as I had not known him, I did not give the matter much thought," I said to them. Then

[159]

one of the men said, "It has been discovered that Peter did it. Do you think that they are right?" "I don't believe a word of it." Then the man continued, "If you continue to say that you do not know anything about this case, I will not let you go home. You shall go wherever Peter goes. We have found out that you were with him, and that is why we have come here. If you do not tell us, you will never come out of prison. Such is the penalty for what you have done. If you tell us, however, you can get away and you will be our witness and can return home." "I want to get home, and whatever I can do to get home, I'll do. About this matter, however, I know nothing. You can speak about what you know and I about what I know. I do not want to be locked up," I said.

We had now come to town. There I was taken to a hotel and asked if I knew the murdered man's brother. I said, "Yes." We went inside, and there we found him. The man greeted me and said, "If you know anything about this affair and confess, we will not lock you up. You will be one of the witnesses. Even if it should turn out that you were one of them, we will not lock you up. I am not deceiving you. This man who is listening to us agrees with me." He continued: "Sam, I am acquainted with your father. He is a fine old man. Even if you were along with Peter, I will not have you locked up, if you confess. It is merely because Peter is a bad man that I want to know it." "He must be telling the truth," said I to myself. "I'm going to tell." I thought that in such a case they would let me go. So I said: "Yes, I know all about it. I saw Peter when he killed the man." "Good," said they. They thanked me. Then the officer took me outside; he took me to jail and said, "The train will soon be ready." Then he went out.

In the jail I found Peter. "What did they say to you?" he asked. "They did not say anything," I said. "They asked me many questions," said Peter. "They asked me whether you had done it, and they said that if I told them, they would let me go home. I told them, however, that I did not know anything." "They asked me very much the same." I then said, "but I also told them that I did not know anything." "That is good, for without witnesses they have only hearsay evidence and they will not be able to hold us," said Peter. "Anyhow, the man we killed was crazy and his brothers hated him. They used to ask me to kill him," continued Peter.

Just then the officer came and said, "Boys, the train is due soon. Get ready." When we were ready he took out some handcuffs and tied us together, and thus we went to the station. The white people looked at us in surprise, called out our names, and asked what the trouble was. Then the train arrived, and we boarded it. We rode all that night and arrived at our destination in the morning. There the officer locked us up in prison. We did not know what to say. After a time I was taken out and brought to the courthouse. There they again questioned me, and a woman, a shorthand writer, took down my answers. I was then told to tell everything again in detail and that as soon as the time for the trial came, I would be freed. When I was through, they took me back and locked me up again, and the other man was taken out. When he returned, he had of course learned what I had done. He was very quiet. Then I said, "Well, you said you were asked to kill him and you also said that they, the brothers of the murdered man, asked others to kill him. If that is so, you did it because you were asked to do so, and you are not to blame. If we can find other witnesses to this fact, we will surely get out." "Indeed, I spoke about the matter because they had locked us up alone. I did not like it. The boys were so boisterous that I thought the others ought to be in jail, too. That is what I was thinking of when I spoke to the officers. Soon they will bring these others here, too, and when we are all here together, it will not be so lonesome." Peter was glad of it. Soon the other two were brought, and the four of us made quite a good deal of noise talking.

§27. *The Character of the Murdered Pottawat-*
tomie

Now it was rumored at this time that the man we had killed had really been somewhat crazy. He was the oldest of three brothers. Their father had been a chief and had possessed much land. Other people had contributed very much money to buy the land. A number of them lived there, and they had put in many crops. Then the father died, and the oldest son drove away all the people. He drove his two brothers away also. There were many horses, and he forcibly kept them as well as many other things. Whenever he heard that any of his brothers was using any of his horses, he used to scold him. When they argued with him, he threatened to shoot them. It was said that he always went around with his gun. For all these reasons his brothers disliked him, it is said, and used to ask the Winnebago to kill him. It was also said that all his white neighbors disliked him. He had over a hundred horses, and they grew wild in the woods. He did nothing all the time but watch them. They were too wild for him ever to get near them. The only use he ever made of them was to own them. Whenever the horses entered a field, they would destroy it completely, and if anything was ever said to him about the matter, he wanted immediately to fight with those who protested. Whenever a person tried to buy one of them, he would ask an extravagant price, and whenever a horse was caught in depredations and he was asked to pay damages, he threatened to shoot the people concerned. He was accustomed to go around barefooted with his gun, it was said. For all these reasons his brothers disliked him and asked some Winnebago to shoot him. These brothers also told the Winnebago how it would be possible to kill him, for he belonged to that group of people who were regarded as invulnerable. It is said that when he fasted, he had gone without food for a whole winter; that he had not resumed eating until spring. In order to kill him, a wooden knife was required. This should be painted red. Then he was to be stabbed. This was the only way of killing him.

Now we thought that with all this evidence against him, we would surely be acquitted.

§28. *Our Prison Life and the Trial*

We were waiting for the spring term of the court. We stayed in prison all winter. I was very tired of it, but I kept that secret because otherwise the other men would be likely to make fun of me. Sometimes I really felt like crying, but I acted as though I did not care at all. I was married at the time I had been imprisoned, and I hungered to see my wife and was in a terrible condition, but I told the others that I did not care in the least. The others were also married, and some of them showed their lonesomeness markedly. Occasionally one of our wives would visit us. The men said that I seemed the only one who did not apparently care. As a matter of fact, of course, I could hardly stand it, although I kept my condition quite secret. I only felt better when I wrote a letter to my wife, and then when she answered I felt very happy.

We used to read one another's letters, and whenever our wives wrote to us, we would tease one another about the contents.

After a while the spring term of the court arrived, and we were happy. When the time for our trial came, however, we were told that our case had been bound over to the fall term. So we had to stay in prison all summer. When the fall term came, the case was bound

[165]

over until the following spring. It was enough to cause one to say "Oh, my!" in impatience. During the winter we used to make bead work and compete with one another as to who could do the best. We made beaded finger-rings, and these were always purchased by some one. By selling these rings we thus made quite a good deal of money. We also made suspenders. I made thirty of them and sold them for seven dollars a pair. We thus had plenty of money and drank all the time. There were some prisoners locked up together with us whose terms were almost over, and these were allowed to go outside. They would buy us the whisky. We gambled, too, playing for money stakes.

One day my wife came to visit me. I talked to her through the iron grating. I was allowed to talk to her for a long time. All I could do was to desire her. I wanted her badly. When the wives of the others came, they felt just as I did.

Once we had a fight. We had been drinking and were disputing about a game. Afterwards we were quite humble about it.

Shortly after this we found out that my wife had married again. I did not feel like eating, but I tried hard to do so, because I thought that the others would notice it. Then I said to them, "I am glad to hear about this report that my wife has married again. When I get out of prison I will pay the one who has married her, for he is taking care of her until my release. Indeed I have felt quite uneasy about her for some time. Now I feel quite relieved, for she is being provided for." Thus I spoke. But the truth of it was that I was as angry as I could very well be. I made up my mind that I would take her away from whomsoever she might be living with. Then I thought that I would make her feel as sad as I could; I thought I would disfigure her, cut off her nose, then take her to the wilderness, give her a sound beating, and leave her there. I could not think of anything else all the time, and I believe that for a time I did not even taste food. I often felt like crying. At night I would not be able to sleep, for I could not forget the whole affair. Sometimes I would dream of seeing her, and then in the morning I would tell the others about it and feel better. Throughout all this time I never thought of all those of my relatives who were really concerned for me. Not even that grateful was I. I only thought of the woman.

Now the time for the next session of the court had arrived. It was the spring session. We were given a trial. They always took us to the court in handcuffs. We had each a lawyer. At the first hearing one of us was freed, the other three remaining in prison. Then the lawyers pleaded the case of the others, and two more were freed, I being one of these. The man who had actually done the killing was the only one who remained in prison.

§29. *My Release from Prison and First Acquaintance with the Peyote*

When we were released we found our relatives waiting for us. My older brother was there, and with him I went home. We began to drink immediately. I was very happy, although when I was in prison I had felt that I would never drink again. We reached the Winnebago the same day. There I met a woman, and I cohabited with her that very night. I had been desiring that for a long time. Then I began to drink again. After a while I went to Black River Falls and there met my former wife, whom I immediately took back again.

The Indians were just then celebrating their midsummer feasts. I went among them, took part, and drank a great deal. I considered myself a brave man and a medicine man; I thought myself a holy man, a strong one, and a favorite with women. I felt that I was in possession of many courting medicines. A brave man I felt myself; a fleet runner. I was an excellent singer of songs at the Brave Dance; [29] I was a sport, and I wanted whisky every day.

My mother and father had gone to the Missouri River, to the Winnebago living in Nebraska. They left me in charge of two horses and a wagon belonging

[29] A non-sacred war dance whose songs were very popular.

[168]

to them for me to use. Later on, in the fall, when the cranberry season had started, I lived with three women. I never did any work, but simply went from woman to woman. Then the annuity payment was made, and I went around chasing the payment. I sold my horses and spent the money I had.

About this time my father and mother asked me to come to Nebraska. I had been told that my father and mother had joined the peyote people and were eating peyote, and I did not like it. These peyote eaters were doing wrong, were wicked, and that is why I disliked them. Old Thunder Cloud, my brother-in-law, told us the following about them:

"This medicine, the peyote,[30] is one of the four spirits from below. That is why it is bad. These four spirits have always longed for human beings, and now they are getting ahold of them. Those who use the peyote claim that when they die, they will only be going on a

---

[30] The peyote is a small cactus common in the state of Chihuahua, Mexico, out of which from time immemorial an intoxicating drink has been prepared. The ancient Mexicans were well acquainted with it. For a number of centuries it has been the center of various cults all of which contained marked Christian features. It is only within the last fifty to seventy-five years, however, that some of these cults have spread into the United States. It is from some of the tribes now living in Oklahoma that the Winnebago borrowed it.

The Winnebago either eat the peyote button in its dried state or drink a concoction prepared from it. The effects are various. Every one, however, seems to be agreed upon its causing wonderful color visions. The after effects vary with the individual. I have seen some practically in a state of stupor after eating a large quantity of the buttons, while others seem entirely unaffected and go on with their day's work as though nothing had happened.

The use of the Bible is an entirely new element introduced by the Winnebago.

long journey. But that is not the truth, for when they eat peyote, they destroy their souls, and death to them will mean complete extermination. If I spit upon the floor, the saliva will soon dry up and nothing will remain of it. This is what death will mean to them. I might go out and preach against this doctrine, but it would be of no avail, for I certainly would not be able to draw more than one or two people away from this spirit who lives below. Many will be taken in by this medicine; they will not be able to help themselves in any way. This bad spirit will certainly seize them."

For all these reasons none of us liked it. However, my parents sent me the money for the trip, and my brother and sisters told me to go. Just before I started, my youngest sister, the one to whom we always listened most attentively, said to me, "Older brother, do not you indulge in this medicine eating, in this peyote." I promised, and then started out for Nebraska.

When I arrived in Nebraska I met some people who had not joined the peyote eaters, and they said to me, "Your relatives are eating the peyote and that is why they sent for you, that you too might eat. Your mother, your father, and your younger sister, they are all eating it." Thus they spoke to me. They also told me of a number of other bad things these peyote people were supposed to have done. I felt ashamed, and I wished I had not come in the first place. Immediately after that I told these people that I was going to eat the peyote.

Soon after that I met my father, mother and sister.

My Release from Prison

They were glad to see me. Then we all walked to their home. My father and I walked by ourselves and he told me about the peyote. "It does not amount to anything, all this that they are doing. Yet those who partake, stop their drinking. Sick people also get well. We were told these things and therefore joined. What they claimed is true and your mother is practically well now; and so am I. They claim to offer prayers to Earthmaker, to God." He stopped and then continued, "The peyote people are rather foolish for they cry when they feel very happy about anything. They throw away all the medicines that they possess and whose virtues they know. They give up all the blessings they received while fasting, give up all the spirits who blessed them. They stop giving feasts and making offerings of tobacco. They burn up all their holy things, destroy the war-bundles. They stop smoking and chewing tobacco. They are bad people. They burn up their medicine pouches, give up the Medicine Dance and even cut up their otter-skin bags.[31] They say they are praying to Earthmaker, to God, and do so standing and crying. They claim to hold nothing holy except Earthmaker, God; that everything they are giving up comes from the bad spirits, that the bad spirits deceived them. They claim that there are no spirits with the power of bestowing blessings and that there is no other spirit except Earthmaker, God." Then I said,

[31] The most sacred object of the Medicine Dance. It is within the otter-skin bag that the shell is concealed with which the newly initiated members of the dance, as well as the regular members, are shot.

[171]

"Say, they certainly talk foolishly." I felt very angry at them. "You will hear them yourself for they are going to have a meeting to-night. Their songs are very strange. They use a small drum," said my father. Then I felt a strong desire to see them.

Finally we reached our home. That night there was to be a peyote meeting. At first I sat outside and listened to them. I grew very fond of them. I was a stranger in their country and the young members of the peyote religion were exceedingly friendly to me. They lent me money occasionally and treated me with tender regard. They did everything that they thought would make me feel good and in consequence I used to speak as though I really liked the ceremony. I was, however, only deceiving them. I only said it because they were so good to me. I thought they acted in this way because the peyote was deceiving them.

Soon after that my parents returned to Wisconsin telling me that they would return in a short time. I was thus left alone with those of my relatives who were peyote followers. That is why they left me there. Whenever I went among the non-peyote people I used to say all sorts of things about the peyote people and when I returned to the peyote people I used to say all sorts of things about the others.

I had a friend who was a peyote man and he said to me, "My friend, I wish very much that you would eat the peyote." Then I answered him, "My friend, I will do it but not until I get accustomed to the people of this country. Then I will do it. What worries me most is the fact that they are making fun of you. Quite apart from that, however, I am not used to them." I was speaking quite dishonestly.

I was then staying at my sister's place. She was a peyote follower and had gone on a visit to Oklahoma. After a while she returned. At that time I was staying with a number of women and from them I obtained money. Once I got drunk and was locked up for six days. After my sister returned she and her friends paid more attention to me than ever before. This was particularly true of her husband. I was given horses and a wagon. I was really treated very tenderly. I told them I believed in the peyote because they treated me so nicely. I knew that they did this because they wished me to eat the peyote. I, in my turn, was very kind to them. I thought I was fooling them and they thought they were converting me.

We moved after a while to a place where there was to be a large peyote gathering. I knew that they had arranged for this in order to get me to join. Accordingly I spoke to my younger sister and said, "Sister, I would be quite willing to eat this peyote ordinarily, but I don't like the woman with whom I am living just now and I think I shall leave her. Now I have been given to understand that among you, when married people eat the peyote they will always have to stay together. I shall therefore join you as soon as I have married a woman with whom I wish to stay permanently." Then my brother-in-law came in and my sister told him what I had said and he spoke to me,

"You are right in what you say. However, the woman with whom you are staying is a married woman and you cannot stay with her any longer. This marriage of yours is null and void and we know that this is so. You had better join now. You are the same as if you were single, and we will pray for you as though you were single. After you have joined the peyote religion you may marry any woman you wish and whom you have a right to marry legally. So, do join to-night. It is best. For some time already have we been desirous of your joining us but we never said anything to you about it. It is Earthmaker's blessing, God's will, that has made you think of this." So he spoke to me.

§30. *I Eat the Peyote*

I sat inside the lodge with them. One man acted as leader and we were to do whatever he ordered. The various objects belonging to the ceremony—the two peyote buttons, the drum, the eagle-wing fan, and the small gourd rattle—were all placed before him. I wanted to sit in some place on the side for I felt that I might get to crying like the others. I felt quite ashamed of myself.

The leader arose and talked. He said that this was an affair of Earthmaker's and that he, the leader, could do nothing of his own initiative; that God was going to conduct the ceremony. He said the medicine, the peyote, was holy and that he would turn us all over to it. He further said, "I am a very pitiful figure in this ceremony so that when you pray to Earthmaker, pray also for me. Now let us all rise and pray to Earthmaker." We all rose. Then he prayed. He prayed for the sick and he prayed for those who did not yet know Earthmaker. He said that they were to be pitied. When he had finished we sat down. The peyote was then passed around. They gave me five buttons and my brother-in-law spoke to me, "If you speak to this medicine, the peyote, it will give you whatever you ask of it. After that you must pray to

Earthmaker and then eat the peyote." I, however, ate the peyote immediately for I did not know what to ask for and I did not know what to say in a prayer to Earthmaker. I therefore ate the peyote buttons just as they were. They were very bitter and had a taste difficult for me to describe. After eating them I wondered a good deal about what was going to happen to me. Soon I was given five more peyote buttons and these also I ate. They tasted rather bitter. I was now very quiet for the peyote had somewhat weakened me. I listened attentively to the singing and liked it very much. I felt as though I were partly asleep and quite different from my normal self. When I looked around and examined myself, however, I saw nothing wrong. I certainly felt different from my normal self. Before this I used to dislike the songs but now I liked them very much, particularly those the leader was singing. I liked listening to him very much.

They were all sitting very quietly and doing nothing expect singing. Each man sang four songs and then passed the sacred objects to the next person. Each man held a stick and an eagle's feather in one hand and a small gourd rattle, which he would shake when singing, in the other. One of the participants did the drumming. In this manner the sacred objects would be passed along until they came back to the leader. The leader would then sing four songs and when he had finished these, place the sacred objects on the ground and rise and pray to Earthmaker. Then he called upon one or two to speak. These people all said

[176]

that Earthmaker was good and that the peyote was good, and that whosoever ate the peyote would be able to free himself from the bad spirit. They said that Earthmaker forbids us to commit sins. When this was over they sang again.

After midnight I would every now and then hear some one cry. In some cases I saw a person go up to the leader and talk to him. He would stand up and pray with him. I was told what these people were saying. I was told that these people were asking others to pray for them for they were sorry for the sins they had committed and wished to be prevented from committing them again. They cried very loudly. I was rather frightened, especially when I noticed that when I closed my eyes and sat still, strange things began to appear before me. I was not in the least sleepy. Then the light of morning came upon me. In the morning, when the sun rose, the ceremony stopped. All got up and prayed to Earthmaker and left.

During the daytime I did not get sleepy in the least. My actions, however, were a little different from my usual ones. Then the people said, "To-night they are going to have another meeting. Let us go over. They say that this is the best thing to do for then, you can learn the ceremony immediately. It is said that the souls of the members of the peyote ceremony wander all over the earth and the heavens. All this you will learn and see." They continued, "At times the members die and remain dead all night and day. When in this condition they sometimes see Earthmaker, it is claimed." Some say that the home of the bad spirit can also be visited when in this state.

So that night we went to a meeting again. I doubted all their claims, of course, and thought that they were untrue. Nevertheless I went along. When we got near I had already eaten some peyote for I had taken three in the day. Now near the place where the peyote meeting was to be held there was a regular Winnebago feast and to that I went instead. I found a long lodge and heard a terrific noise. An enormous drum was being beaten. The sound almost raised me in the air so pleasurably loud did it sound to me. Not so pleasurable had things appeared at the peyote meetings that I had lately been attending. There I danced all night and I flirted with the women. I left about day and when I reached the peyote meeting it was still going on. When I got back I was told to sit in a certain place and I was treated very kindly. There I again ate peyote. I also heard that they were going to have another meeting nearby on the evening of the same day. We continued eating peyote at the place where we were staying, which was the house of one of my relatives. Some of the boys taught me a few songs and they said, "Say, when you learn how to sing you will be the best singer, for you are a good singer as it is. You have a good voice." I thought so myself.

§31. *The Effects of the Peyote*

That night we went to the place where the peyote meeting was to be given. I was given a place to sit down and treated very kindly. "Well, he has come," they even said to me when I came, "make room for him." I thought they regarded me as a great man. John Rave, the leader, was to conduct the ceremony. He told of his conversion:

John Rave's Conversion to the Peyote Religion

During the years 1893 and 1894 I was in Oklahoma among the peyote eaters.

There one night, in the middle of the night, we were to eat peyote. I also ate some. Then later on in the night I got frightened for a living thing seemed to have entered me. "Why did I do it?" I thought. "I should not have done it for right at the beginning I have harmed myself. Indeed I should not have done it; I am sure it will injure me. The best thing for me to do will be to vomit it up. Well, now I am going to try it." After a few attempts I gave up. I thought to myself, "Well, now you have done it! You have been going around trying everything and now you have succeeded in doing something that will harm you. What is it? It seems to be alive and moving around in my stomach. If only some of my people were here! That

[179]

would have been much better. Now, no one will know what became of me; I have killed myself."

Just then the object within me seemed to be coming out. It seemed almost out and I put my hand in my mouth to feel it, but then it went back again. "Oh my! I should never have done it at the very start. Never again will I do it. I am surely going to die!"

So we continued and then day dawned and I laughed. Before that I had been unable to laugh.

The following night we were to eat the peyote again. I thought to myself, "Last night it almost harmed me." "Well, let us eat the peyote again," the people said and I answered, "All right, I'll do it." So we ate seven peyote apiece.

Suddenly I saw a big snake. I was very much frightened. Then another one came crawling over me. "My God! Where are these snakes coming from?" There at my back there seemed to be something also. So I looked around and saw a snake about to swallow me entirely. It had legs and arms and a long tail. The end of its tail was like a spear. "O God! I am surely going to die now," I thought. Then I turned in another direction and I saw a man with horns and long claws and with a spear in his hand. He jumped for me and I threw myself on the ground. He missed me. Then I looked back. This time he started back but it seemed to me that he was directing his spear at me. Again I threw myself on the ground and he missed me. There seemed to be no possible escape for me. Then it suddenly occurred to me, "Perhaps it is the peyote that is doing this to me? Help me, O Medicine, help me! It is you who are doing this and you who are holy! Not these frightful visions are causing this. I should have known that it was you, indeed, who were doing it! Help me!"

The Effects of the Peyote

Then my suffering stopped. "As long as the earth shall last, that long will I make use of you, O Medicine!"

This had lasted a night and a day. For a whole night I had not slept.

Then we breakfasted and when we were through I said, "Let us eat peyote again to-night." That evening I ate eight peyote.

In the middle of the night I saw God. To God living up above, our father, I prayed. "Have mercy upon me! Give me knowledge that I may not say and do evil things. To you, O God, I am trying to pray. Do thou, O Son of God, help me too. This religion, let me know this religion!" Thus I spoke and sat very quiet. Then I beheld the morning star and it was good to look upon; the light was good to look upon. I had been frightened during the night but now I was happy. Now as the light appeared it seemed to me that nothing would be invisible to me. I seemed to see everything clearly. Then I thought of my home and as I looked around there I saw the house in which I lived far away among the Winnebago. It was quite close to me. There at the window I saw my children at play and I saw a man going to my house carrying a jug of whisky. Then he gave them something to drink and the one who had brought the whisky got drunk and annoyed the people. Finally he ran away. "So this is what they are doing?" I thought to myself. Then I beheld my wife. She came out and stood outside the door wearing a red blanket. She was thinking of going to the flag pole and was wondering which road to take. "If I take this road I am likely to meet some people, but if I take the other, I am not likely to encounter any one."

Indeed it is good. They are all well—my brother, my sister, my father, my mother. I felt very good indeed. O

Medicine, grandfather, most assuredly you are holy! All that is connected with you, that I would like to know and that I would like to understand. Help me! I give myself up to you entirely!

For three days and for three nights I had been eating the peyote and not slept at all. Now I realized that throughout all the years that I had lived, I had never once known a truly holy thing. Now, for the first time, I knew it. Would that some of the Winnebago might also know it!

Many years ago I had been sick and it looked as if this sickness were going to kill me. I tried all the Winnebago doctors and then I tried all of the white man's medicines, all were of no avail. I thought to myself, "You are doomed. I wonder whether you will be alive next year?" Such were the thoughts that came to me. As soon as I ate the peyote, however, I got over my sickness. After that I was not sick again. My wife suffered from the same disease and I told her that if she ate the peyote it would cure her. She was afraid although she had never seen it before. She knew that I had used it and yet was afraid. Her sickness, however, got worse and worse and one day I said to her, "You are sick. It is going to be very difficult but try the peyote anyhow. It will ease you." Finally she ate it. I had told her to eat it and then wash herself and comb her hair and that she would get well. She got entirely well. I painted her face and took my gourd and began singing to her very much. Then I stopped. "Indeed, you are right," she said, "for now I am well." From that day to the present she has been well. Now she is very happy.

A man named *Black-waterspirit* was having a hemorrhage at about that time and I wanted him to eat the peyote.

The Effects of the Peyote

"Well," said he, "I am not going to live anyhow." "Eat the peyote nevertheless," I said, "and you will get cured." Before that consumptives never were cured and now for the first time one was cured. *Black-waterspirit* is living to-day and is very well.

Then there was a man named *Walking-priest*. He was very fond of whisky, chewed, smoked, and gambled. He was also terribly addicted to women. Indeed he did everything bad. I gave him some of the peyote and he gave up all the bad things he was doing. He had a very dangerous disease. He even had murder in his heart. To-day he is living a good life. Such is his desire.

Whoever has any evil thoughts, let him eat the peyote and he will lose all his bad habits. It is a cure for everything bad.

To-day the Winnebago say that only God is holy. One of the Winnebago told me this: "Really the life that I led was a very bad one. Never again will I do it. This medicine is good and always will I use it." *John Harrison* and *Squeaking-wings* were prominent members of the Medicine Dance; they thought much of themselves, as did all the members of the Medicine Dance. They knew all the secrets of the ritual. Both of them were gamblers and were rich because they were gamblers. Their parents had acquired great wealth by giving medicines to the Winnebago. These two men were very rich and believed that they had a right to be selfish with their possessions. Then they ate the peyote and ever since that time they have been followers of the peyote. They were very ill at one time and now they have been cured of their illness. Now if there are any men who can be taken as examples of the workings of the peyote, it is these three I have mentioned. Even if a man were blind and had only heard of these three men he would realize that if any medicine is good it is this one. It is a cure for all evil.

Before I thought that I knew something but really I knew nothing. It is only now that I have real knowledge. In my former life I was like one blind and deaf. My heart ached when I thought of what I had done. Never again will I do it. This medicine alone is holy, has made me good and rid me of all evil. The one whom we call God has given me this. That I know positively. Let them all come here; men and women; let them bring with them all that they desire; let them bring with them their diseases. If they come here they will get well. This is all true; it is all true. Bring whatever desires you possess along with you and then come and eat or drink this medicine. This is life, the only life. Then you will learn something of yourself. Come with your disease for this medicine will cure it. Whatever you have, come and eat this medicine and you will have true knowledge once and for all. Learn of this medicine yourself through actual experience.

If you just hear about it you are not likely to try it. If you desire real knowledge you must partake of it for then you will learn of things that you had never known before. In no other way can you ever get happy. I know that all sorts of excuses will run through your head for not partaking of it, but if you wish to learn of something good, try it. Perhaps you will think to yourself that it will be too difficult and this will seem a good excuse for not trying it. Why, however, should you do this? Even if you partake of only part of the good claimed, yet I know that you will say to yourself, "Well, this life is good enough." After you have taken it for the first time, it will seem as if you were digging a grave for yourself with it, that you were about to die. Indeed you will be wondering what was going

[184]

The Effects of the Peyote

to happen to you. The coffin will be set before you and you will see your own body. If you wish to inquire further about where you are going you will discover something that you had not known before. Two roads there are, one leading to a hole in the earth and the other extending above. You will learn something that you had not known before. Of the two roads, one is dark, the other is light. You must choose one of these while you are alive and you must decide therefore whether you wish to continue in your evil ways or whether you intend to abandon them. These are the two roads. The peyote people see them. They claim that only if you weep and repent will you be able to attain knowledge. Do not, as I said before, listen to others talking about this medicine, but try it yourself. That is the only way to find out. No other medicine can accomplish what this has done. If, therefore, you make use of it, you will live. People who have eaten peyote throw aside all the evil ceremonies that they performed before. Only by eating the peyote will you learn what is truly holy. That is what I am trying to learn myself.

It is now twenty-three years since I ate the peyote and I am still doing it (1912). Before that, my heart had been filled with murderous thoughts. I wanted to kill my brother and my sister. It seemed to me that my heart would not feel good until I killed one of them. All my thoughts were fixed on the warpath. That is all I thought of. Now I know that this was all caused by the evil spirit that possessed me. I was suffering from a disease. I even desired to kill myself; I did not care to live. That feeling too was caused by this evil spirit dwelling within me. Then I ate the peyote and became attached to them and I wanted them to live.

This the medicine had accomplished.

When John Rave had finished I ate five peyote.
Then my brother-in-law and my sister came and gave
themselves up. They asked me to stand there with
them. I did not like it, but I did it nevertheless.
"Why should I give myself up? I am not in earnest
and I intend to stop this as soon as I get back to
Wisconsin. I am only doing this because they have
given me presents," I thought. "I might as well get
up, however, since it doesn't mean anything to me."
So I stood up. The leader began to talk and I suddenly began to feel sick. It got worse and worse and
finally I lost consciousness. When I came to, I found
myself lying on my back. Those with whom I had
been standing were still there. As a matter of fact,
I had regained consciousness as soon as I fell down.
I felt like leaving the place that night but I did not
do it. I was quite tired out. "Why have I done
this?" I said to myself. "I promised my sister that I
would not do it." So I thought and I tried to leave
but I couldn't. I suffered intensely. At last day
dawned. Now I thought that they regarded me as
one who had had a trance and had seen something.

Then we went home and they showed me a passage
in the Bible where it said that it was a shame for any
man to wear long hair. I looked at the passage. I was
not a man learned in books, but I wanted to give the
impression that I knew how to read so I told them to
cut my hair. I was still wearing it long at the time.
After my hair was cut I took out a lot of medicines,
many small bundles of them. These and my shorn hair

The Effects of the Peyote

I gave to my brother-in-law. Then I cried and my brother-in-law also cried. He thanked me, told me that I understood and that I had done well. He told me that Earthmaker alone was holy; that all the blessings and medicine I possessed were false; that I had been fooled by the bad spirit. He told me that I had now freed myself from much of this bad influence. My relatives expressed their thanks fervently.

On the fourth night of my stay they had another meeting and I went to it again. There I again ate peyote. I enjoyed it and sang along with the others. I wanted to be able to sing immediately. Some young men were singing and I enjoyed it so I prayed to Earthmaker and asked him to let me learn to sing right away. That was all I asked for. My brother-in-law was with me all the time. At that meeting all the things I had given my brother-in-law were burnt up.

Now the fact that my brother-in-law had told me that I understood, had pleased me and I felt good when daylight came. As a matter of fact, I had not received any knowledge at all. I thought, however, that this was the proper way to act, so I did it. After that, I would attend meetings occasionally and I looked around for a woman whom I cared to marry permanently. Before long that was the only thing that I would think of when I attended the meetings.

§32. *I Am Converted*

On one occasion we were to have a meeting of men and women and I went to it with a woman, the one with whom I thought I would go around the next day. That was the only reason I went with her. When we arrived at the meeting, the leader asked me to sit near him and there I was placed. He urged me to eat many peyote and I did so. Now the leaders of the ceremony always place the sacred objects in front of themselves. The sacred peyote was also placed there. Now the one this particular leader placed in front of himself this time was a very small one. "Why does he have a very small one?" I thought to myself. However, I did not think of this matter long.

It was now late at night. I had eaten a lot of peyote and felt rather tired. I suffered considerably. After a while I looked at the peyote, and there I saw an eagle standing with outspread wings. It was as beautiful a sight as could well be observed. Each of the feathers seemed to have a mark. The eagle stood there looking at me. I turned my gaze, thinking that perhaps there was something the matter with my sight, but then when I looked again the eagle was still present. Again I turned around and when I looked at the spot where the eagle had stood, it was gone and only the small

I Am Converted

peyote remained. I then watched the other people, but they all had their heads bowed and were praying.

Suddenly I saw a lion lying in the same place where before I had seen the eagle. I watched it very closely and when I turned my eyes for the least little bit, it disappeared. "I suppose all those present are aware of this and I am just beginning to find out," I thought. Then I saw a small person at the same place. He wore blue clothes and a shining brimmed cap. He had on a soldier's uniform and was sitting on the arm of the person who was drumming, scrutinizing everybody. He was a little man but perfect in all proportions. Finally I lost sight of him. I was very much surprised indeed. I sat very quietly. "So this is what it is," I thought. "This is what they all probably see and which I am just now beginning to find out."

Then I prayed to Earthmaker, to God:

"This, your ceremony, let me hereafter perform!"

§33. *I See God*

As I looked again I saw a flag. I looked more carefully and I saw the house full of flags. They had the
most beautiful marks on them. In the middle of the
room there was a large flag, a living one. It was moving. In the doorway there was another one not entirely
visible. I had never seen anything so beautiful in all
my life before.

Again I prayed to God. I bowed my head and closed
my eyes and began to speak. I said many things that
I would ordinarily never have spoken about. As I
prayed I was aware of something above me and there
He was, He to whom I was speaking, God. That which
we call the soul, that it is which is God. This is what
I felt and saw. The one called Earthmaker, God, is a
spirit and He it was I felt and saw. At least this is
what I learned. I instantly became their spirit; I was
their spirit or soul. Whatever they thought of I immediately knew. I did not have to speak to them and get
an answer to know what their thoughts were. Then I
thought of a certain place far away, and immediately
I was there. I was my thought.

I looked about and watched the people around me
and then when I opened my eyes I was myself in body
again. From now on thus it shall be, I felt. This is

the way they are and I am only now beginning to find out. "All those who heed God must be thus. I shall not need any more food for am I not my spirit? I shall have no more use of my body; my corporeal affairs are over." Thus I felt.

Then all stopped and left the lodge, for it had begun to dawn. Some one spoke to me. I did not answer, for I thought they were just fooling and that they were like myself, that therefore it would be unnecessary for me to speak to them. So instead of speaking I answered with a smile. "They are just saying this to me because they realize that I have only now found out," I thought. That was why I didn't answer. I did not speak to any one until noon. Then I had to leave the house to urinate and some one followed me. It was my friend. He said, "My friend, what troubles you that makes you act as you do?" "Well, there's no need of your saying anything, for you know it beforehand," I said. After saying this I got over my trance and was restored to my normal condition. My friend had to speak to me before I knew his thoughts. I became like my former self.

Then I spoke to him and said, "My friend, let us hitch up the horses and then I will go wherever you like, for you wish to speak to me and I also want to speak to you." I continued, "If I were to tell you all that I have learned, I should never be able to stop, so much have I learned. Yet I shall gladly tell some of it." "Good," said he. He liked what I told him very much. "I am anxious to hear what you have seen," he said. We went to look for the horses and caught one of them. The other had wandered far away and we could not find it. We hunted everywhere but could not locate it.

§34. *Visions*

Now ever since that time, no matter where I am, I always think of this religion. I still remember it and I think I shall remember it as long as I live. It is the only holy thing that I have become aware of in all my life.

After that, whenever I heard of a peyote meeting, I went to it.

My thoughts, however, were still always fixed on women. "If I were married legally, perhaps these thoughts would leave me," I thought. Whenever I went to a meeting, therefore, I tried to eat as many peyote as possible, for I was told that it was good to do that. I always prayed to Earthmaker as I sat there. Such were my thoughts. "If I were married," I thought, "then I should be able to put all my thoughts on this ceremony." I sat with my eyes closed, very quiet.

Suddenly I saw something. It was an object all tied up. The rope with which this object was tied up was long and the object itself was running around and around in a circle. A road was present in which it ought to have gone, but the object was so tied up that it was unable to reach it. The road was an excellent one. Along its edge grew blue grass and on each side grew many varieties of pretty flowers. Sweet-smelling flowers sprang up all along its path. Far off in the distance appeared a bright light. There a city was visible, of beauty indescribable. A cross was in full sight. The object tied up would always just fall short of reaching the road. It seemed to lack sufficient strength to break loose from whatever it was that was holding it. Nearby lay something that would have given it sufficient strength to break its fastenings if it were only able to get there.

I looked at what was so inextricably tied up and I saw that it was myself. I was forever thinking of woman. "This it is with which I am tied," I thought to myself. "Were I married I would have strength enough to break my fastenings and be able to travel in the good road." Then daylight came upon us and the ceremony stopped.

Then I thought of a man I used to know, an old peyote man. He always spoke kindly to me. I went over to see him. I thought that I would tell him what had happened to me. He was very glad and told me that I was speaking of a very good thing. Then finally he said, "Now I shall tell you what I think is a good thing for you to do. You know that if an old horse is balky, you cannot break him of this habit; even if you had bought him and tried to break him, you would not succeed. If, indeed, you had succeeded, it would only be after very hard work. However, if you had a young horse, you could train it in any way you wished. So it is in everything. If you marry a woman who has been in the habit of getting married frequently, it would be difficult for her to break herself of the habit she loved. You are not the one she loves. If you marry her, you will lead a hard life. If you wish to get married, take your time. There are plenty of good women. Many of them are at government schools and have never been married. I think you would do best if you waited for some of these girls. They will return in the middle of summer. So don't think of any of these women you see around here, but wait until then and pray to God patiently. That will be the best, I think." I liked what he told me and thanked him. I decided to accept his advice, and I did not look around for women after that. I was to wait for about three months and during that time I paid strict attention to the peyote ceremony.

On one occasion while at a meeting, I suffered great pain. My eyes were sore and I was thinking of many things. "Now I do nothing but pay attention to this ceremony, for it is good." Then I called the leader over to me and said to him, "My elder brother, hereafter I shall only regard Earthmaker as holy. I will make no more offerings of tobacco. I will not use any more tobacco. I will not smoke, nor will I chew tobacco. I have no further interest in these things. Earthmaker, God, alone do I desire to serve. Never again shall I take part in the Medicine Dance. To you do I give up myself completely. I intend to give myself up to God's cause." Thus I spoke to him. "It is good, younger brother," he said to me. Then he had me stand up and he prayed to God. He asked God to forgive me my sins.

The next morning I was taken home. My eyes were sore and I could not see. They took me back to my house and there they put a solution of the peyote in my eyes and I got well in a week.

One night when I was asleep I dreamed that the world had come to an end. Some people God took while some belonged to the bad spirit. I belonged to the bad spirit. Although I had become a peyote man I had not as yet been baptized. That was why God did not take me. All those who belonged to God were marked, but I was not. I felt very bad about it when I woke up, even although I had only dreamed it. I felt very bad indeed. I wanted them to hurry and have another peyote meeting soon. I could hardly wait until I reached the place where the next meeting was to take place. I immediately told the leader what I wanted and asked him to baptize me and he baptized me in the morning. After that I felt better.

Then I went to work and I worked with a railroad work gang. I was still working when the time for the midsummer celebration approached. I always went to the peyote meeting on Saturday nights.

The old man was right in what he had told me. The girl students returned in the summer. Shortly after they returned, a man, a friend of mine, who had gone around with me, asked me if I wanted to get married. "Yes, I do," I answered. Then he said, "Listen, I have been thinking of something. What kind of a woman do you wish to marry?" I told him what I had in mind. Then he said, "Come home with me. I have a younger sister; I want her to marry a good man; I would like to have her marry you." Then I went home with him. When we reached his home and discussed the matter, the girl gave her consent. The parents also consented. So there I got married, and what I expected has taken place and I have lived with her ever since. On one occasion, after she was used to me, she told me this: Before she had married, she had determined that, if she ever got married, she would not care to marry a very young man. "I wanted a man who ate peyote and who paid attention to the ceremony." Such a man she desired and such a person she said I was. She loved me and she was glad that she had married me. This is what she had asked God for in her prayers. "And indeed it has happened as I wished," she said. She believed that it was the will of God that we had done this. Together we gave ourselves up to the peyote at a meeting. From that time on we have remained members of the peyote religion.

§35. *I Have a Strange Experience*

Many things are said under the influence of the peyote. The members get into a kind of trance and speak many things. On one occasion they had a peyote meeting which lasted two nights. I ate many peyote. The next morning I tried to sleep. I suffered a great deal. I lay down in a very comfortable position. After a while a fear arose in me. I could not remain in that place, so I went out into the prairie, but here again I was seized with this fear. Finally I returned to a lodge near the one in which the peyote meeting was being held, and there I lay down alone. I feared that I might do something foolish to myself if I remained there alone, and I hoped that some one would come and talk to me. Then some one did come and talk to me, but I did not feel any better. I went inside the lodge where the meeting was taking place. "I am going inside," I told him. He laughed, "All right, go in." I went in and sat down. It was very hot and I felt as though I was going to die. I was very thirsty, but I feared to ask for water. I thought that I was certainly going to die. I began to totter over.

I died and my body was moved by another life. I began to move about and make signs. It was not myself doing it and I could not see it. At last it stood up. The eagle feathers and the gourds, these it said, were holy. They also had a large book there. What was contained in that book, my body saw. It was the Bible. The sacred objects were not holy, but they were good ornaments. My body said that if any one paid attention to God's ceremony, he would be hearkening to what the Bible said. God's Son said that He was the only way. This means that one can only live from the word. My body spoke of many things and it spoke of what was true. It spoke of all the things that were being done by the Winnebago and that were evil. It spoke a long time and then stopped. Not I, but my body standing there, had done the talking. I should be confessing myself a fool if I were to think that I had said all this, my body told me.

After a while I returned to my normal condition. Some of the people present had been frightened thinking that I had gone crazy. Others, on the other hand, liked it. It was discussed a good deal; they called it the "shaking" state. It was claimed that the condition in which I had been was not part of God's religion. I was told that whoever ate a lot of peyote would, through the peyote, be taught the teachings of God. God's ways and man's ways are different. Whoever therefore wished to help this religion must give himself up to it. If you eat a good deal of the peyote and believed that it could teach you something, then it assuredly would do so. That, at least, is the way in which I understand this matter.

Once we had a meeting at the home of a member who was sick. The sick would always get well when a meeting was held in their home and that is why we used to hold them there. At this particular meeting I got into the shaking condition again. My body told us how our religion was an affair of God's and how even if one knew only a portion of it, one could still partake of it. Thus it spoke. "God, His Son, and His Holiness, these are the three ways of saying it. Even if you know one of these three, it means all. Every one of you has the means of opening the road to Earthmaker. It is given to all of you. With belief you can open the door to God. You cannot open it with knowledge alone. How many letters are there to the *key*, to the road? Three. What are they? "There were many educated people present, but none of them said anything. "The first letter must be *K*." If, therefore, a person said *K*, that would be the whole of it. "But let me look into the Bible and see what it means," said the body. Then the body took the Bible and began turning the leaves. The body did not know where the passage was itself. Finally in Matthew, Chapter 16, it stopped. There it speaks about it. "Peter did not give himself up," it says. "For a long time he could not give up his own knowledge." There, in that passage, it says Key. That is the work of God. At least, so I understand it. He made use of my body and acted in this manner in the case of the peyote.

At one meeting O. L. spoke about the old stories. He spoke as follows:

I Have a Strange Experience

The old people often spoke of the Trickster, but we never knew what they meant. They told us how he wrapped a coonskin blanket around himself and went to a place where all the people were dancing. There he danced until evening and then he stopped and turned around. No one was to be seen anywhere and then he realized that he had mistaken for people dancing the noise made by the wind blowing through the reeds.

So do we Winnebago act. We never look before we act. We do everything without thinking. We think we know all about it.

The Trickster was walking around with a pack on his back. As he walked along, some one called to him: "Say, we want you to sing." "All right," said he. "I am carrying songs in my pack and if you wish to dance, build a large lodge for me with a small hole at the end for an entrance." When it was finished, they all went in and the Trickster followed them. Those who had spoken to him were birds. He told them that while dancing they were not to open their eyes, for if they did, their eyes would become red. Whenever a fat bird passed the Trickster, he would choke it to death, and if it cried out, he would say, "That's it! That's it! Give a whoop!"

After a while, one of the birds got somewhat suspicious and opened its eyes just the least little bit. He saw that the Trickster was choking all the birds. "He is killing us all," said the bird. "Let all who can, run for their lives." Then he flew out through the top of the house. The Trickster took the birds he had killed and roasted them, but he did not get a chance to eat them, for they were stolen from him.

So are we Winnebago. We like all that is forbidden. We say that we like the Medicine Dance; we say that it is good and yet we keep it secret and forbid people to witness it. We tell members of the dance not to speak of it until the world shall come to an end. They are afraid to speak of it. We, the Winnebago, are the birds, and the Trickster is Satan.

Once, as the Trickster was going along the road, some one spoke to him. He listened and he heard it say, "If any one eats me, all bad things will come out of him." Then the Trickster went up to the one talking and said, "What is your name?" "My name is *Blows-himself-away*." The Trickster would not believe it; so he ate the thing. After a while he blew himself away. He laughed. "Oh, pshaw! I suppose this is what it meant." As he went along it grew worse and worse and it was only after the greatest hardship that he succeeded in returning home.

So are we Winnebago. We travel on this earth all our lives and then when one of us tastes something that makes him unconscious, we look upon this thing with suspicion when he regains consciousness.

From that time on I go about everywhere telling every one that this religion is good. Many other people at home said the same thing. Many, likewise, have joined this religion and are getting along nicely.

On one occasion after I had eaten a good deal of peyote, I learned the following from it; that all I had done in the past had been evil. This was plainly revealed to me. What I thought was holy, and by thus thinking was lost, that I now know was false. It is false, this giving of pagan feasts, of holding the old Winnebago things holy, such as the Medicine Dance and all the other customs.

§36. *Finale*

I have written about all these matters and I have spoken out very clearly in all I have told you. I talked to the older people when you first asked me to get this information for you, but they refused to do it. I thought I would write down and tell you all these things so that those who came after me would not be deceived.[32] Then you asked me to obtain this information for you and in this I was aided by my brother and by O. L.

Before I joined the peyote I went about in a most pitiable condition, and now I am living happily and my wife has a fine baby.

This is the work predestined for me to do. This is the end of it.

[32] This is the reason I gave when trying to induce the Winnebago to give me information.

APPENDIX

Paul Radin's publications in the field of Native American autobiography extend from 1913 to 1945, and include Jasper Blowsnake's "Personal Reminiscences of a Winnebago Indian" (1913); Sam Blowsnake's "The Autobiography of a Winnebago Indian" (1920); Thundercloud's monologue in Parsons, "Thunder-Cloud, a Winnebago Shaman, Relates and Prays" (1922); the many autobiographical narratives in *The Winnebago Tribe* (1913, 1923); the expansion of Sam's "Autobiography," *Crashing Thunder* (1926); and, finally, some autobiographical fragments from Jasper Blowsnake in *The Road of Life and Death* (1945), an account of the Winnebago Medicine Rite. Radin seems to have collected all the material on which these publications were based in the years 1908–13, when he worked among the Winnebagos.

Many of Radin's field notes and transcriptions from this period have been preserved and are among the papers donated by his widow, Doris Radin, to the American Philosophical Society Library in 1960. These are catalogued in John F. Freeman, *A Guide to Manuscripts Relating to the American Indian in the Library of the American Philosophical Library* (Philadelphia, 1966). Among these is an item listed as "Sam Blowsnake's Autobiography" (Freeman, #3897). This consists of three lined "American Chief" notebooks (yellow covers, with a picture of an Indian, bow in hand, and three tepees in the background), numbered 30, 31, and 32, and filled with pencil script in the Winnebago language. Each notebook is dated October 9, 1913, and each is marked, on the cover, "Jasper Blowsnake's Autobiography," with the name Jasper crossed through in pen, and the name Sam written above it. Whose markings are these? Did Radin himself have trouble keeping Sam and Jasper apart in his mind? Unlike many of the other manuscripts in the Radin collection, these notebooks do not have interlinear or facing-page translations, and I cannot read Winnebago. Are these notebooks all or part of S.B.'s own manuscript? And what is actually in them? A transcription and translation of "Sam Blowsnake's Autobiography" is only one of the tasks that remain for the student of *Crashing Thunder* and of Paul Radin's work in Native American autobiography.

A comparison of the autobiographical texts Radin published between 1913 and 1945, together with an examination of his papers in the American Philosophical Library collection reveal instances of what appear to be the multiple attribution of materials, of overlappings of materials, and—most clearly of all—changes in the published versions of apparently similar materials over the years. In what follows I attempt to provide a guide to the major and representative instances, one that selectively focuses on the composition of *Crashing Thunder* so as to bear upon the issues of textuality, literariness, and scienticity raised in the Introduction.

In the 1913 "Personal Reminiscences," Jasper Blowsnake provides no account of his fasting experiences; in *The Winnebago Tribe* (*WT*), however, there is a monologue called "J.B.'s Fasting Experience." This begins, "I fasted all the time. We moved back to a place where all the leaders used to give their feasts. Near the place where we lived there were three lakes and a black hawk's nest . . . (*WT*, 308). The third chapter of Sam's 1920 "Autobiography" (A) is called "Fasting." Its second paragraph begins, "After a while we got fairly well started on our way back. I fasted all the time. We moved back to a place where all the leaders used to give their feasts. Near the place where we lived there were three lakes and a black hawk's nest . . ." (A, 6). This is supposed to be Sam; but his account parallels, detail for detail, and almost word for word, the account ascribed to J.B.; this is carried over into *Crashing Thunder* (*CT*, 17–20) with only a few changes. If this account actually derives from Sam, it is unclear why Radin would have assigned it to Jasper in *The Winnebago Tribe*. That it does indeed come from Sam is suggested by a series of undated manuscript notes Radin made for a commentary on the "Autobiography" (Freeman, #3881) in which he comments on Sam's fasting experience.

In the fifth of these manuscript notes, Radin remarked that "Blowsnake's account of his puberty / fasting is not told in a very coherent fashion, and is at times vague and careless. . . . That he should say that he made his appeal to the spirits when the sun rose

Appendix

seems strange to me for that is the moment when one is generally supposed to stop fasting. Blowsnake, I think through an oversight, uses the word for Thunderbirds instead of spirits here." This is consistent with Radin's footnote in the "Autobiography" that Sam's fasting experience in its "supernatural" details was "peculiar in a number of respects" (A, 7 n.). (There is no similar note accompanying the account in *Crashing Thunder*.) Radin's manuscript notes also comment that

> the fasting experience given here differs considerably from the one told me by Blowsnake's older brother and which was also supervised by his father. This raises the important question of what it is Blowsnake is giving here and whether this is even approximately what his father had told him. These are difficult questions to answer. My impression is that Blowsnake is probably combining here what his father had told him with the fasting experiences of others, particularly of his brother-in-law [Thundercloud]. It should be remembered that *he himself had not had the experience he here records* and this would permit secondary embellishment to creep in more easily. [My emphasis]

We are left, thus, with several questions. Why did Radin assign Sam's fasting experience (as I suspect he did) to J.B. in *The Winnebago Tribe*? If the fasting experience Sam narrated or wrote down was not one he had actually had, but, instead, a composite, replete with "secondary embellishment," why didn't Radin, in the introductory material and notes to the "Autobiography" and *Crashing Thunder*, permit "the important question of what it is Blowsnake is giving here" to surface? Further, if Sam's experience is in some regards "peculiar," how does that observation accord with Radin's purpose, as stated in the introduction to the "Autobiography," of having "some *representative* middle-aged individual . . . describe his life in relation to the social group in which he had grown up" (A, 2, my emphasis)? (In *Crashing Thunder*, the apparently representative Sam has become a quite extraordinary rake [*CT*, x], a decidedly "definite personage" [A, 2]—yet still doing duty as the "real" Indian.)

The issue of representativeness and uniqueness, of the conflation of personal, historical experience with collective and conventional experience in a tribal culture is presented as well by Radin's expansion of the "Fasting" chapter of the "Autobiography" for *Crashing Thunder*. In *Crashing Thunder*, Radin added the stories "Crashing Thunder's" father had told him of his ancestors Weshgishega and Jobenangiwinxga. The story of Wecgicega comes from chapter 1 of the "Personal Reminiscences" (PR), "How One of My Ancestors Was Blessed by Earth-Maker." There, Jasper's account reads, "Wecgicega they called him. A Winnebago he was. When he was grown up, his father coaxed him to fast; (saying) that when Earth-Maker created the various spirits, as many good spirits as he made, all of them did he place in control of something" (PR, 294). In *Crashing Thunder*, not Jasper's but Sam's autobiography, we have "Fasting: The Story of My Ancestor Weshgishega": "When Weshgishega was growing up his father coaxed him to fast. He told him that Earthmaker had created the various spirits, all the good ones he had created, were placed in charge of something" (*CT*, 20).

Another version of this material appeared in an unidentified monologue in *The Winnebago Tribe* called "How Wegi'ceka Tried to See Earthmaker." It begins as follows: "Once there was a Winnebago whose name was Wegi'ceka. As soon as he was grown up his father begged him to fast. The old man told his son that Earthmaker, when he created this earth, made many good spirits and that he put each one of them in control of powers with which they could bless human beings" (*WT*, 291). Radin's note explains that "some religious experiences" of the Winnebago "have been cast in a literary form and handed down from one generation to another. The literary mold in which they have been cast does not in the least interfere with their value as excellent examples of personal experiences" (*WT*, 292 n.). This parallels Radin's note in the "Personal Reminiscences" that the Wecgicega story "is really a favorite story among the Winnebago" (PR, 294 n.) and may or may not actually refer to one of Jasper's historical ancestors. But the interaction of literary convention and individual "personal experience" is a much more complicated matter than Radin allows for. If, as is altogether possible, three different informants (Jasper, Sam, and an unidentified Winnebago) told the same story, in approximately the same words, mingling traditional motifs with their own historical experience, this would be interesting to know. On the other hand, Radin's tendency to attribute a single narrative

Appendix

to several different narrators may make one wary. I would remark, too, that if Sam Blowsnake has here told the same story as Jasper and another Winnebago, in this instance he appears coherent, precise, and careful in the transmission of traditional material.

Speaking of his brother-in-law Thunder-Cloud, in the "Personal Reminiscences," Jasper said, "He had lived once long ago, had joined the Medicine Dance and had strictly adhered to all its precepts. A good man he was; no one did he dislike; never did he steal; and never did he fight" (PR, 303). "Crashing Thunder's" version in 1926 (this did not appear in the 1920 "Autobiography") reads, "Thus my brother-in-law had lived long ago, had joined the Medicine Dance and adhered strictly to its precepts. He was a good man; he disliked no one; he never stole and never did he fight" (CT, 7). Jasper's conclusion was, "For all these things, I used to love my brother-in-law. Never did I show any disrespect to him" (PR, 312). "Crashing Thunder's"—Sam's—conclusion reads, "My brother loved Thunder Cloud for these reasons" (CT, 14). The brothers may well have related the same facts—but, again, did they use exactly the same, or nearly the same, words? In *The Road of Life and Death* (RLD), Jasper is presented as saying, "For all these things, I loved my brother-in-law. Never did I show any disrespect toward him" (RLD, 4). But there Radin drops out a paragraph written by Jasper in which he testifies that "now that [he is] a Peyote follower," he knows "there was no foundation to what [Thunder-Cloud] said" (PR, 312). Obviously the dramatic quality of the Medicine Rite would be undercut by explicit statement of its falsity. "Crashing Thunder's" comments on the falsity of the old ways are also saved for much later in his account. These changes are Radin's.

Thunder-Cloud's own fasting experiences appeared in the middle of chapter 3 of the "Personal Reminiscences": "Then he [Thunder-Cloud] told of his fasting experience" (PR, 306). There follow some three pages of first-person monologue in quotation marks (i.e., Thunder-Cloud is represented as speaking for himself and in his own words). Thunder-Cloud's narrative is exactly the same as the one that appears in *The Winnebago Tribe* as "Thunder-Cloud's fasting experience" (WT, 275–76). (This is also introduced by the unassigned sentence "Then he [Thunder-Cloud] told of his fasting experience.") Radin footnotes it, in the "Personal Reminiscences," "This is the fasting experience told by all those who have been blessed with shamanistic powers" (PR, 306 n.). This fasting experience is not given for Thunder-Cloud by Sam in his "Autobiography," although *Crashing Thunder* does contain a portion of the same fasting experience (*CT*, 8–9), this time with changes in the wording that did not appear before. Apparently this is one of the "things" "Crashing Thunder" told Radin "on previous occasions . . . inserted in its proper" place (*CT*, preface, xi). Or, on the other hand, could it be something told Radin by Thundercloud, or something written by Jasper Blowsnake attributed to Sam?

Radin added to chapter 3, "Fasting," of the "Autobiography" the story of "Crashing Thunder's" brother J.'s blessing. Page 8 of the "Autobiography" reads, "Just then my older brother came home and they objected to his return for he had not been blessed." *Crashing Thunder* repeats this (27), but adds, "My brother J., however, obtained a blessing." There follows a third-person, shortened version of the first-person narrative called "Account of J.'s fasting" in *The Winnebago Tribe* (293–95). Who is J.? There were three Blowsnake brothers, and *The Winnebago Tribe* prints narratives from both J. and J.B. If J. spoke or wrote the account of his fasting given in *The Winnebago Tribe*, was it also repeated verbatim by Sam? It would be interesting to know, for the answer might aid our understanding of the transmission of traditional materials in an oral culture also using written forms.

Similar confusions, overlappings, and multiple attributions occur in Radin's various presentations of the climactic moment in each of the Blowsnake brothers' lives, the moment of their conversion to the Peyote religion. The monologue titled "J.B.'s Peyote Experiences" in *The Winnebago Tribe* (400–412), is almost word for word the same as chapters 28–34 of Sam's "Autobiography." Peyote conversions by this time had a certain tradition among the Winnebagos and individual conversions may have followed a conventionalized pattern. Nonetheless, it seems hard to believe that Jasper and Sam can have had exactly the same experiences (especially, as I note just below, when other, quite nontraditional experiences are assigned to both of them), and can have narrated them in exactly the same words. Connected with but not strictly a part of the conversion experience of the Blowsnakes is a murder that both of them are alleged to have committed. In "J.B.'s Account of his Conversion" in *The Winnebago Tribe* (412–14), an

Appendix

account that is carried into *The Road of Life and Death* (46–49), Jasper—apparently—says, "I was at the old agency. There they were to try me for murder." Sam's arrest and trial for the murder of a Potawatomi is presented in some detail in the "Autobiography" (41–47) and in *Crashing Thunder* (148–51, 159–67) and is referred to by Mountain Wolf Woman, his sister (*Mountain Wolf Woman*, 100, 124); but only in this particular monologue is there any indication that Jasper also was in jeopardy for murder. It seems hard not to conclude that this is simply a multiple attribution, the result of carelessness—or some other reason of which I am not aware.

Radin's treatment of Sam's conversion to the Peyote religion in the "Autobiography" and in *Crashing Thunder* is interesting to consider. In chapter 30 of the "Autobiography," "The Effects of the Peyote," Sam writes, "John Rave, the leader, was to conduct the (ceremony)" (A, 55–6). The thirty-first chapter of *Crashing Thunder* has the same title and repeats the sentence I have just quoted. But whereas the "Autobiography" continues, "I ate five peyote" (A, 56) *Crashing Thunder* inserts, "He [John Rave] told of his conversion" (*CT*, 179). There follows a lengthy narrative called "John Rave's Conversion to the Peyote Religion" (*CT*, 279–85). A modified translation of "John Rave's Account of the Peyote Cult and of His Conversion" in *The Winnebago Tribe* (*WT*, 389–94), this occurs as "John Rave's peyote experience" in the Radin manuscript collection (Freeman, #3878), with an interlinear translation. Both the version in *The Winnebago Tribe* and that in *Crashing Thunder* have claims to accuracy when compared with this rough translation, although they are stylistically different.

This insertion into the text of *Crashing Thunder* makes Sam's account of his converison much more dramatic than it was in the "Autobiography," for here we are given John Rave not only leading the Peyote ceremony but also testifying, at that particular ceremony, to his own conversion. In *Crashing Thunder*, it is only after Rave's narrative that Sam announces, "When John Rave had finished I ate five peyote" (*CT*, 186). There is at least the implication that Rave's powerful story may have operated as a cause of S.B.'s own conversion. To the extent that this is so, it is Radin, not Sam Blowsnake, who has produced this effect, for it occurs only in *Crashing Thunder*. This part of *Crashing Thunder*, I would add, appears, therefore, to be a fiction; John Rave's account is, no doubt, authentic, and Sam Blowsnake, no doubt, heard it on one occasion or another—but probably not on this occasion, else its omission from the "Autobiography" is inexplicable.

I save for final—and brief—mention the very many small changes Radin made in the titles and arrangements of chapter headings and of the wording as he went from the "Autobiography" to *Crashing Thunder*; whether these are significant, and the particular significance one attaches to them, must depend upon a given interpreter's particular outlook. For example, chapter 4 of the "Autobiography" is "Boyhood Reminiscences"; chapter 4 of *Crashing Thunder* becomes "Reminiscences of Childhood." In 1920, the nineteenth chapter is "Continued Dissipation"; in 1926 this becomes the twenty-first chapter, called "Dissipation." Changes of this nature tell me very little. On the other hand, I would remark the fact that chapter 14 in 1920 is called "Brother's Death," while the same chapter, now the eighteenth of *Crashing Thunder,* becomes "My Brother Is Murdered," a more dramatic title.

I have already commented in the Introduction on Radin's changes in the "Finale" of *Crashing Thunder,* where the "Autobiography's" sentence "This is the work that was assigned to me" (A 67) became "This is the work predestined for me to do" (*CT*, 203). The brief "Finale" has many other changes of this sort. As Nancy Lurie has noted (*Mountain Wolf Woman,* 98), Radin deleted the "Autobiography's" phrase "Then my brother had us do this work" (A, 67). Lurie offered no explanation for this deletion; my own conjectures in these regards have been covered in the Introduction. There are a very great many such changes, large or small; to catalog and comment on them is part of the work that remains to be done.

INDEX

[213]

Index